THE CAREER RESOURCE LIBRARY

Careers
in

Alternative Medicine

Alan Steinfeld

The Rosen Publishing Group, Inc.
NEW YORK

Published in 1997, 1999, 2003 by The Rosen Publishing Group, Inc.
29 East 21st Street, New York, NY 10010

Revised Edition 2003

Cover Photo by Alan Steinfeld

Library of Congress Cataloging-in-Publication Data

Steinfeld, Alan, 1956–
Careers in alternative medicine/by Alan Steinfeld.
  p. cm.
Includes bibliographical references and index.
ISBN 0-8239-3754-2(lib. bdg.)
1. Holistic medicine—Vocational guidance. 2. Alternative medicine —
Vocational guidance. 3. Alternative medicine—Study and teaching—
United States—Directories. 4. Holistic medicine—Study and
teaching—United States—Directories. I. Title.
R733.S854 1996
610.69—dc20   96-22638
        CIP
        AC

Manufactured in the United States of America

C ontents

Introduction

When this book was first written, people interested in unorthodox alternative medicine were barely accepted in our society. Now, five years later, in this third edition, we see that what were once considered alternatives have become mainstream. These conglomerates of healing systems are currently so popular in the United States that they have a standard acronym: CAM for complementary/alternative medicine. The newly formed White House Commission on Complementary and Alternative Medicine has policies that define the scope and practice of complementary and alternative medicine (CAM) and recognizes that these practices "continue to evolve."

At one end of the spectrum, there are full systems of therapies, such as acupuncture and massage, that operate professional schools, publish journals and textbooks, have local, state and national organizations, and subscribe to codes of ethical practice. Other less professional, but very powerful, methods of healing include aromatherapy and iridology. They have a less systematized course of development. These are often used to supplement fuller systems for diagnosis and healing. In addition, there are new forms of healing that emerge every year, such as vortex healing or Su Jok.

Definitions

According to the World Health Organization (WHO), the term "alternative medicine" means any form of medicine that is outside the mainstream as practiced by the majority of doctors today. Among these other forms of treatment, there are more than 100 systems of alternative medicine in practice today, some of which are hundreds or even thousands of years old. Every country has its own native system of health care. China has acupuncture; France, magnetic healing; India, Ayurveda; Japan, shiatsu; and various Muslim countries, Unani.

In 2002, the Medical Subject Headings Section of the National Library of Medicine classified alternative medicine under the term "complementary therapies." This text defined therapeutic practices as those not currently considered an integral part of conventional allopathic (disease treatment) medical practice. Specifically, "complementary" is used in addition to conventional treatments and "alternative medicine" is used when a therapy is performed instead of a conventional treatment.

In this book, I sometimes use the terms alternative medicine, complementary medicine, and CAM interchangeably. There are other names that refer to similar therapies that are beyond most conventional medicine. They pretty much all refer to the same thing. Some of these terms are:

Traditional medicine is a form of medicine that has been practiced by ancient cultures around the world and has been handed down from generation to generation. Many involve herbal cures.Two-thirds of the world's population (mainly in developing countries) rely entirely on such treatments.

Holistic medicine, also called mind-body, is what most alternative medical systems really are. Its practitioners consider the human body as a complete being, composed of physical, mental, social, and spiritual dimensions that all need to be treated.

Ethno medicine, also called folk medicine, is traditional health care closely associated with the life and culture of a certain population. It is interesting that even where Western medical care is available to people in developing countries, the majority remain loyal to its indigenous medical systems.

Natural medicine involves methods based on the laws of nature and natural substances.

Integrative medicine is now becoming the preferred term. Many doctors that are combining Western medical practices with a broad range of healing therapies such as herbology and/or energy healing simply refer to their practices as integrative medicine. They claim that integrative medicine provides the best of both approaches. In addition, many health clinics now have medical doctors, acupuncturists, massage therapists, and chiropractors working side by side.

The term "integrative" marks a great achievement in the long road to acceptance for CAMs. The World Health Organization said, "For far too long traditional systems of medicine and modern medicine have gone their separate ways in mutual antipathy. Yet are not their goals identical—to improve the health of mankind and thereby the quality of life? Only the blinkered mind would assume that each has nothing to learn from the other."

Order of Development

Surveys have found that many people seek out conventional medical treatment first, and then turn to CAM practitioners. Most people appear to use CAM in conjunction with, not as a replacement for, conventional medical therapy, and many seek out care that integrates the best of a variety of approaches. The use of CAM models, practices, and products by the general population ranges from 6.5 percent to 42 percent. Other studies have documented even higher uses of CAM therapies among people with chronic and life-threatening conditions. For example, a recent study at a major cancer center indicated that 69 percent of patients included CAM approaches as part of their cancer care.

Getting the Most from This Book

As the demand and interest in alternative medicine increase by a public weary of high medical costs and non-curative techniques, students are finding a growing job market. The number of massage and acupuncture schools and classes on herbal remedies has grown to literally thousands in the last few years. Opportunities are everywhere for the eager practitioner who is well educated, prepared, and ready to help others. A career in this field means dealing with individuals and their physical and lifestyle needs. This work also requires a certain type of temperament.

The underlying theme of this book is healing. In addition to preparing yourself to enter the field of alternative medicine, you should seek a well-rounded approach to health care that includes an integration of science and alternatives.

This Book's Structure

The earlier editions of this book included ancient therapies, such as acupuncture, as well as newly invented forms, such as crystal healing. In this edition, however, after the explosion of pop healing arts in the 1980s and 1990s, it appears that the cream has risen to the top, and what is left are those therapies that have survived public scrutiny and remain most vital and effective.

Part 1 discusses the basic background of alternative health care. It will also ask you to examine your own beliefs about health and healing.

Part 2 examines the multitude of options available to study in the alternative health care field. As you read this section, take notes of the therapies that attract you the most. Then go back and investigate the schools and organizations that you are most interested in. Some treatment modalities overlap, so once you have a general sense of the type of work you want to pursue, it is important to follow up.

This section is further divided into two parts. The first portion deals with therapies that require professional training and long years of study. The second part examines those therapies that are mostly supplementary, for which courses are given over a shorter period of time, even a weekend.

Part 3 is devoted to the future of the field. Alternative medicine is taking on an increasingly vital role in our society. Therefore, the demand for practitioners is growing. This section also discusses the business aspect of the field.

Responsible Member of Society

You will find that all therapeutic approaches are holistic. This is the idea of treating the whole person, integrated in mind, body, and spirit. In contrast, most Western medical education focuses on the intellect, leaving out the mind-body connection.

Alternative medicine encourages the individual to play an active role in his or her own well-being. It also stresses prevention as a primary goal rather than focusing solely on the treatment of a disease. By gaining a deeper education in complementary and alternative therapies, you will be better able to help yourself and others. Whether you choose to work as a health care professional or are studying to be of service to friends and family, these natural therapies will empower you to become a proactive participant in your own health. As you prepare to enter the field of alternative medicine, you should seek a well-rounded approach to health care that includes an integration of science and the spirit of healing.

Part I
Why Consider Alternatives?

CAM's Growing Popularity in the United States

A decade ago, the American health care system was facing a crisis in patient care. Antonia C. Novello, the surgeon general at the time, said that a "symptom of the situation was that we have come to accept levels of chronic disease as normal. The medical system is failing to address many health concerns of the population."

The Chinese word for "crisis" also means opportunity. It is interesting that at approximately the same time that health care in the United States was considered to be in crisis, alternative and complementary medicine was making a huge advance in popularity. It is no coincidence that the crisis/opportunity of the 1990s gave the American public a reason to seek alternatives to the conventional medical establishment for their health care needs. Today, mainstream media reports attest to the widespread use of complementary and alternative medicine.

One of the champions of the alternative health care movement has been Senator Tom Harkin of Iowa. He has been instrumental in creating public recognition and federal funds for research in alternative and comple-mentary medicine. In a major speech to the American public he said:

> Ten years ago, when I first started working on this issue, things were very different. Studies showed that a lot of people were using CAM reme-dies, but no one was talking about it. It was often publicly dismissed as quackery, and the medical community frowned upon it. I knew that I wanted to bring CAM out into the open. I wanted to pro-vide for research and examination. Today, 60 per-cent of physicians have referred patients to CAM practitioners. In addition 64 percent of U.S. med-ical schools offer courses in CAM and 80 percent of medical students and 70 percent of family physi-cians want training in CAM therapies. More and more medical-pioneers like Dr. Jim Gordon are integrating alternative medicine with mainstream practices. More and more medical schools like the University of Iowa are teaching alternative medi-cine right along with conventional medicine.

> This is just what Americans are looking for. They want less invasive, less expensive, less impersonal medical treatment. They want reme-dies that are safe, holistic, and affordable. They want to be involved in their own health care. They want medical practitioners to listen to them and to think of them as a whole person, not just an entity with an illness. Most of all, they want medicine that works, whether it's old or new, run-of-the-mill or out-in-left-field, traditional or alternative.

Health Care Today

The crisis is far from over. The costs of doctors and hospitals are still overwhelming and there are still many resources that the mainstream medical world is not embracing. However, in many cases, health care is now being met in a complementary way allowing doctors and alternative medical practitioners to work together and embrace the benefits of both.

Conventional medicine has had many benefits. People are living longer today than in the past. This is due in part to the cure and prevention of infectious disease. Conventional medicine excels in the management of bacterial infections, acute trauma, childbirth emergencies, treating broken bones, performing corrective surgery, and treating acute, life-threatening illnesses.

However, many illnesses treated with drugs and surgery could be treated more effectively with less toxic and less invasive measures. Illnesses that are self-limiting, meaning they pass on their own, like the common cold, are often overtreated with prescription medications, because patients and doctors are used to treating health problems this way. Many conventional medical treatments address health problems that could have been prevented through lifestyle changes and then tackle symptoms without addressing the cause of the illness. This is a reflection of the fact that conventional medicine tends to view the human body as a biological machine and disease as a breakdown of that machine. The focus is often on repairing individual parts of the machine. This view fragments the body into parts and loses sight of the whole person. Some scientists and doctors believe that the overuse of antibiotics in the last forty years has contributed to the development of bacteria that are increasingly resistant to treatment. This, along with added stress and a greater presence of toxins in our food, air, and water, all has contributed to the crisis.

Today, alternative medicine and holistic therapies are often celebrated for bringing humanism back into patient care. They are no longer a hope for the future but are instead a reality that is being more readily embraced by physicians, health care workers, and a significant proportion of the general public. Health and living naturally, once considered merely fads, have become a permanent lifestyle for many.

On the National Front

In 1992, the Office of Alternative Medicine (OAM) was established within the National Institutes of Health (NIH) to evaluate alternative health treatments and to integrate effective ones into mainstream medicine. Within its operating budget of \$4 to \$13 million, over 300 different alternative approaches were researched, identified, categorized, and evaluated. As a result of positive evaluations by the OAM, on October 21, 1998, President Bill Clinton signed a bill upgrading the office to the National Center for Complementary and Alternative Medicine (NCCAM).

While the OAM's primary role was rigorous scientific evaluation of CAM treatments, NCCAM is concerned with supporting research, training, and providing a clearinghouse for information to the public. This is an important move on a national and local level, for it creates another level of legitimacy for alternative medical therapists. With a budget of only

15

$50 million, less than one-half of 1 percent of the total NIH budget, NCCAM will help broaden the visibility of complementary and alternative medical modalities.

Underlying NCCAM's programs is a congressional mandate to disseminate information to practitioners and the public and to set up and carry out programs that further investigate complementary and alternative medical treatments. NCCAM evaluates CAM practices such as acupuncture, as well as the safety and efficacy of widely used natural products, such as herbal remedies and nutritional and food supplements. It provides information about the nature and principles of CAM systems and sponsors scientific research about CAM practices for health professionals and the public.

When looking into different modalities, make sure to use the governmental research for your own benefit. Get a fact sheet from the NCCAM Clearinghouse, the agency designed to give you a quick overview of NCCAM efforts to advance CAM research. The NCCAM Clearinghouse also provides general information about complementary and alternative medicine and, in some cases, includes the names and telephone numbers of more in-depth resources. NCCAM Clearinghouse responds to inquiries in English and Spanish.

NCCAM Clearinghouse
P.O. Box 7923
Gaithersburg, MD 20898
(888) 644-6226
(866) 464-3615 (for the hearing impaired)
e-mail: info@nccam.nih.gov
Web site: http://nccam.nih.gov

The Development of Medicine

Many alternative healing methods come directly from ways of healing that have been practiced for thousands of years and that are still practiced by people around the world. The systems of healing developed by different cultures reflect each culture's individual philosophy and way of viewing the world. Thus, the countries of the Western world have types of medicine that differ in many ways from those of India, called Ayurveda, or the system developed in China.

Shamans, Herbalists, Healers

Anthropologists suggest that shamanism was the earliest form of medicine. It is believed that all modern medicine has its roots in this tradition. Shamanic cultures see illness as belonging to the unseen—the spiritual world. In these cultures, a wide variety of healing rituals and practices were developed to deal with certain forms of illness. The shaman, a medicine man or woman, performs rituals and ceremonies designed to influence the patient's inner feelings and to help him or her stimulate the natural healing powers that all living organisms possess. The shaman does this sometimes by entering an extraordinary state of perception (or reality) and making contact with the spirit world. Then, on behalf of the patient, the shaman releases the spirit, or solves the spiritual problem that caused the illness.

In early societies, there was no separation between the practice of medicine and the practice of religion. In most cases, the shaman was the priest or priestess as well as the medicine man or woman of the society. This ancient system, which continues today in parts of China, India, and Africa, is at the root of current holistic healing. The shamanic concept of health is that the human being is an integral part of the order of the universe. Shamanic therapies help restore the harmonious relationship between a person and the spiritual world. The focus of the shaman is less on physical illness and more on the treatment of the emotions and spiritual well-being of the patient. For instance, one of the oldest texts on Chinese medicine says that the lowest form of medicine heals physical problems. The next level maintains health, but the highest form of medicine connects people to their destiny, their reason for living.

Plants as Medicine

It can be substantiated that in all cultures native plants were used as the first means to heal specific ailments. The first record of this dates back at least 5,000 years, but the oral traditions go back for thousands of years before that.

In 1991, the body of a man, preserved in ice and estimated as being 5,300 years old, was discovered in the Italian Alps. With him was a leather pouch that contained natural antibiotics made from the fruit of a birch fungus. Research indicated that the "iceman" had a parasitic infection that the fruit was helpful in combating. The British medical journal *The Lancet* reported that "the discovery of the fungus suggests the Iceman was aware of his intestinal parasites and fought them with measured doses."

In the book *The Man in the Ice*, archaeologist Dr. Konrad Spindler writes, "All folk medicine has its origins in prehistory. Over hundreds and thousands of years, remedies were passed on from generation to generation. The modern pharmaceutical industry has frequently analyzed the active ingredients of traditional medicines and makes use of them to this day when synthetic forms cannot be produced." Archaeologists have also discovered hieroglyphics in the tombs of the ancient Egyptians. When deciphered, the hieroglyphics were shown to include lists of at least 300 herbs, one-third of which are still in use today.

Shamanism and herbology are often referred to as folk medicine. Folk remedies are practices that have been orally passed down from generation to generation. Many of these healing methods are still used to treat the majority of people around the world. According to the World Health Organization (WHO), 80 percent of the world's population relies on the traditional medicine of their culture.

The Hippocratic Tradition

The roots of Western medicine can be traced directly back to the Greek physician Hippocrates, who lived around 400 BC. Before Hippocrates, the Greeks prayed to the goddesses Hygeia and Panakeia for health and healing. Hygiene and panacea, which means a remedy for all ills, are derivatives of these Greek names. Hygeia was concerned with the maintenance of health, whereas Panakeia specialized in the knowledge of herbs and plants. The bacteriologist René Jules Dubos wrote about this tradition in his 1959 *Mirage of Health*: "For the worshipers of Hygeia the most important feature of medicine is to discover and teach the natural laws which ensure a man a healthy mind in a healthy body." Healing rituals were conducted by priests called Asclepiads ("sons of Asclepius"). Asclepius was the father of Hygeia and Panakeia, and his wife, Epione, was the soother of pain.

The name Asclepius comes from Chaldean, the language of ancient Babylon. Asclepius means "snake-instructing-man." Snakes symbolize regeneration because of their ability to shed their skins. Asclepius was always pictured carrying a caduceus, a staff with a snake coiled around it, a symbol that is still associated with medicine.

Hippocrates came out of the Asclepian tradition. He disregarded superstition and rituals and began the science of medicine. For this he is called the "father of medicine." He wrote volumes of books explaining what he had learned from the Asclepian priests, but he added his own insights into the cause and effect involved in the nature of health and healing. His methods differed from the ancient priests in that he believed illness was not caused by spirits but was a natural phenomenon that could be studied and influenced by therapeutic procedures. He understood that medicine should be based on the wise management of one's life and the prevention of illness.

Hippocrates observed that there was a force inherent in all living organisms that he called "nature's healing power." He believed that the role of the physician was to diagnose a problem and to assist in creating favorable conditions for the process of healing. This is the original meaning of the word "therapy." It comes from the Greek *therapeum*, which means "to attend." He saw the role of the physician as that of an attendant or assistant to the natural healing process.

Two of Hippocrates' famous sayings are *Primum non nocere* ("First, do no harm") and *Vis medicatrix naturae* ("Honor the healing power of nature"). He believed that maintaining health involved hygiene, a calm and balanced mental state, a proper diet, a sound work and home environment, and physical exercise.

Galen, Paracelsus, and Pasteur

The physician Galen (AD 131–200) was the next person to have a major influence on Western medicine. Galen adopted and simplified many of Hippocrates' diagnostic methods (discovering what was wrong with the body) and theories of the body. Galen reduced the Hippocratic idea of individual care to a formulaic style of treatment.

Greek physicians believed that illness was caused by an imbalance in bodily fluids called humors. They determined four humors: blood, phlegm (mucus), yellow bile, and black bile. Galen believed that once a physician diagnosed a particular humor imbalance, he needed only to prescribe the proper medication to counteract it.

21

In the mid-sixteenth century, medicine took another turn. Paracelsus, a self-professed alchemist and inventor, developed the idea that it was not the herbs themselves (their physical structure) that contained curative powers, but rather the chemicals inside those herbs. By this Paracelsus meant to demonstrate that the parts of plants (their chemical composition) were greater than the whole (the plant itself). Although Paracelsus recognized the self-healing properties of the body, he publicly opposed the herbal traditions of Hippocrates and Galen.

Paracelsus developed chemical extracts from minerals and isolates, the active ingredients distilled from plants to treat patients. He also sometimes advocated ingesting toxic chemicals to purify the body. He thought that to purify precious minerals, such as gold and silver, caustic minerals were used. He deduced that the same was true of the human body and that taking substances like mercury would purge the body and restore it to health. His view of chemically formulated medicine deeply influenced the development of drugs in the West.

Another major development occurred in the middle of the nineteenth century. French physician Louis Pasteur popularized the idea that microbes (germs) were responsible for disease. A competing theory held that microbes became a threat only if the conditions of the body were susceptible to them and that by keeping the internal environment of the body healthy, these potential agents of infection were ineffectual. Pasteur is said to have supported the latter opinion toward the end of his life.

The Parts Versus the Whole

The approach of science and medicine in the last 200 years reduces everything to what is purely observable by human senses. This has been called mechanism. In this view, the world is seen as a machine, a ticking clock that is winding down. Life is an anomaly in the universe, "a glorious accident," a term coined by neo-Darwinist Stephen Gould. The only way to treat an illness with this philosophical understanding is to give a pill to change the chemistry or perform surgery to alter the physical form. Living organisms are regarded as nothing more than complex machines governed by the laws of physics and chemistry.

There is no understanding in this model of the body's innate intelligence for self-healing. Doctors know that it exists, but most mainstream scientists have no viable philosophy in understanding this. Therefore Western medicine has fallen into understanding the different parts. Doctors specialize in areas of the body and recommend other areas to other specialists. But in reality, the body is whole where all the parts are always interacting and influencing each other.

James Gleick, the author of *Chaos*, wrote in 1987 that "fifteen years ago science was headed for a crisis of increasing specialization." He declared, "Scientists took it for granted that the complex system made up of billions of components must also be different." Studies were getting more and more isolated and more dead ends were being reached. Dramatically, specialization has reversed. Now all areas of study are "turning back a trend in science... and believe they are looking for the whole."

The Holographic Paradigm

What is happening is called a shift in paradigms. A paradigm is a framework of thought (from the Greek word *paradigma* for "pattern"). A paradigm involves something that was there all along but eluded perception because of a lack of understanding. In the development of Western medicine, the doctors who tried an unorthodox treatment were considered quacks and charlatans by their contemporaries until their theories proved true over time. This happened to many medical pioneers, such as Joseph Lister and Louis Pasteur. Even Hippocrates was ostracized when he broke from the Asclepian tradition.

The emerging paradigm can be called the holographic or holistic paradigm. In this model, the body is seen as one aspect of a greater whole called the universe. The whole is more than the sum of its parts and yet each part contains the whole. Life is not a matter of survival but is predicated on a growing awareness of self and others. Humans and life itself are viewed as a reflection and an integral part of everything that goes on in the universe. For example, as we breathe out, the carbon dioxide from our breath is used by plants, which in turn give us oxygen.

With this way of thinking, a practitioner of alternative medicine can focus on one part of the body and still respect and treat the whole person. An iridologist looks at the eyes for information about the internal organs. A reflexologist rubs the feet to ease tension in every muscle.

Energy in Healing

Another aspect of the new paradigm is the importance of the "life energy" in the healing process. This energy has been called by many names in different traditions, including "vital life force" in homeopathy, "innate intelligence" in chiropractic, *chi* in Chinese medicine, and *prana* in the Ayurvedic tradition. Alternative healing methods often focus on restoring balance of this energy within the person's physical system. Generally, alternative medicine views illness as the result of internal or external influences affecting a person's energy. In traditional Chinese medicine, for example, acupuncture, herbs, and massage are all used to re-establish the smooth flow of *chi* throughout the whole person.

Holistic Medicine

To become familiar with holistic medicine, it is important to understand some of the central ideas upon which it is based. Dr. Yeshe Donden, the physician to the Dalai Lama of Tibet, has said: "Health is the proper relationship between the microcosm, which is man, and the macrocosm, which is the universe. Disease is a disruption of this relationship."

Holistic medicine looks at the whole of one's life. Health and disease are byproducts of all aspects of one's life: nutrition, career, mental frame, family and social activities, and spiritual life. If one area is weakened, all areas begin to suffer. If a person is unhappy at work, it will affect all other areas of life.

Disease Versus Illness

The word "disease" defines itself. Dis-ease means not at ease, the inability to be at ease or relaxed. The name of a disease is usually a label that conventional medicine uses to identify the site of a problem. For example, tonsillitis is an inflammation of the tonsils. In alternative medicine, however, illness is viewed as something that affects the whole body, not just its components. Curing a disease means fixing a part, whereas healing an illness involves a whole person.

Resolving illness may require people to make significant changes in their lives. Illness may offer people a chance to examine issues and conflicts in their lives that they might otherwise have ignored. From this perspective, illness can be viewed as an opportunity for growth and personal development, rather than as a problem.

Symptoms are the body's response to illness. Fever is a response to infecting bacteria and viruses. If the fever is reduced too quickly, the body's natural mechanism is thwarted, and the immune system is weakened.

The word "symptom" comes from the Greek word for "signal." A symptom is the body's way of saying it needs help. It is like a light on the dashboard of a car that illuminates to warn that something is wrong. In holistic thinking, the source of the symptom is investigated so that the condition can be addressed. When the condition heals, the symptoms will disappear.

Healing

Many illnesses today are "lifestyle" illnesses, caused by addictive consumption of tobacco, alcohol, and junk food. It has been proven that toxins in our food and in our environment contribute to the majority of illnesses in most of the United States and Canada. These conditions fragment our body, mind, and spirit. Albert Einstein said that you cannot solve any problem from the same level of reasoning that created it. In order to heal, you must change the way you feel.

The results of many recent studies indicate that emotions significantly influence the immune system. Dr. Candace Pert, formerly with the National Institute of Mental Health, found that neuropeptides, chemicals within the brain associated with feelings of anger, sadness, love, and hate, are also present in vital immune system organs. This suggests that there is a connection between emotional states and immune response. Similarly, depressed patients often have elevated levels of cortisol, which can suppress the immune system. Dr. James Gordon, head of the Center for Mind-Body Medicine in Washington, D.C., says that the anatomical connections are indeed apparent and that we are hardwired to respond physically to that which affects us emotionally.

Staying Healthy

Many illnesses are self-limiting, meaning that they pass on their own. Alternative medicine recognizes this fact and believes that health usually occurs spontaneously when conditions for health exist. Therefore, once you become ill, getting healthy again requires the same input that is needed to keep you healthy.

Dr. Leon Chaitow, a doctor of naturopathy and osteopathy in London, says, "To regain health once it has been lost, we need to reverse some, and ideally all, of those processes which may have negatively impacted us. This includes taking responsibility for stopping those lifestyle choices which we know are harmful, whether this is smoking, alcohol, or drugs." Chaitow explains that "our bodies know what we need as long as they [are kept] healthy. Once we begin to take responsibility for ourselves and our bodies, health will follow naturally and spontaneously. We must look at changing our diet, getting exercise, and keeping away from toxic substances."

Health

The World Health Organization states in the preamble to its charter, "Health is a state of complete physical, mental, and social well-being and not merely the absence of disease or infirmity." Even though virtually everyone knows what it is like to feel healthy, it is hard to convey in words beyond "a general sense of well-being." When a person is healthy, his or her body's defense mechanisms and immune system can effectively handle most of the hazards life presents.

Health is not a static state, since the physical body must constantly adapt itself to a changing world. If you are healthy and suffer harm, be it a bruise or a broken bone, you will start healing immediately, since a healthy body has a natural ability to repair itself. You make new skin cells every day. The cells of your digestive system are constantly turning over as a natural part of the process of digestion and excretion.

Our bodies are constantly trying to achieve internal balance. This helps us move through a dynamic physical environment. In this light, temporary phases of illness can be seen as the body's attempt to adjust to new conditions, such as a change in seasons. A temporary phase of ill health can be used for the organism to grow and learn. True health can be seen as a state of dynamic balance.

Wholeness

The word "health" is derived from the Anglo-Saxon term *hale*, meaning "whole." So "to be healed" is "to be made whole"—whole in the sense of who we are as physical, mental, and emotional beings. Health is far more than the absence of disease. Helping someone feel whole can take many forms. It could be a process of touch to help someone relax, or listening to someone who may be upset about a problem at home.

Holism represents a philosophical perspective on the integration of body, mind, and spirit, and depends on obedience to natural laws. Deviation can result in illness. "Good medicine" is a Native American term for anything that makes someone feel better. Good medicine could be a joke or a hug or a walk in the woods.

Wellness

Well-being occurs when one's inner and outer worlds are in harmony. It is related to your interaction with the environment. Your beliefs, attitudes, and perceptions shape the state of health of both your body and your mind. If you have a balanced diet but your thoughts are toxic, the biochemistry of your body will be negatively affected.

Aside from the importance of keeping the body properly nourished and rested, you should also allow minor illnesses to run their course. The National Wellness Institute divides wellness into six categories: physical, social, emotional, intellectual, spiritual, and occupational. Wellness is a dynamic process of making choices every day that will enhance well-being. Being well is a moment-to-moment process of participating in life in an aware and conscious manner.

Elements of Holistic Therapies

Alternative medicine includes many systems of healing, each with its own merits. There are, however, some common features which differentiate them from conventional medicine.

1) They consider the health of a person on a physical, mental, social, and spiritual level, whereas conventional medicine treats the body as a machine.
2) They stress the maintenance of healthy lifestyles, proper diet, exercise, human relations, sexuality, positive attitudes, clean environment, and moral and spiritual values.
3) The preventive aspect of health is given major importance. They strive for a timely diagnosis, early intervention, and treatment. The person is encouraged to participate in his or her total health.
4) Many traditional systems of medicine have answers to diseases to which doctors have found no amenable answer from conventional medical treatment.

5) They emphasize understanding the cause of illness and use noninvasive means and the patient's inherent recuperative abilities as part of the treatment.

6) They understand stress on the immune system is both internal and external, such as the emotions and the environment.

7) They are aware of unnecessary barriers in the therapist-patient relationship.

The Art of Healing

Healing is an art because it is a subjective practice. No one method works for everyone. A practitioner skilled in a particular modality sees each person differently. If you consult a practitioner of Chinese medicine about edema (retention of fluids), one practitioner may find that the source is in the spleen. Another who has studied the same system might find the cause in the kidney or the lungs. In the healing arts, both diagnoses can be correct. Both of these practitioners, if they are good, will treat you effectively, and your edema will disappear, even though their diagnoses differ. Their aim of wellness and balance is the same.

How can this be? The answer lies in the basic approach of the healing arts which involve examining and treating the whole person from a subjective point of view rather than fixing the symptoms with some pre-scribed formula. Quantum physics has shown that the presence of the observer changes the outcome of an experiment, suggesting that no truly objective view of the world is possible. Therefore no two therapists will treat anyone in exactly the same way. Every acupuncturist, massage therapist, and chiropractor will follow his or her own methods for achieving the same results of good health. A good practitioner will bring about healing if possible and will also recognize the limits of his or her method in treating a patient.

The Role of the Health Care Provider

If you choose to become a health care provider, you will be engaging in a career in which your role as an educator will be vital. You will be responsible for telling people about their bodies—how they function and react—as well as instructing patients on how to take better care of themselves and gain a better understanding of their health.

It will be up to you to educate patients about the nature and meaning of an illness and the possibilities of changing patterns in their lifestyles that may have led to the condition. This method of health care is in fact very similar to the original use of the term "doctor," which comes from the Latin word *docere*, meaning "to teach."

Helping someone heal means pointing out any behavior that may be getting in the way of a healthier life. In most cases, some change is needed to help a person heal. This change can be in behavior or movements, internal or external. However, people may be resistant to change. A person with a chronic sore throat due to smoking may have a difficult time quitting smoking. Ideally, a therapist will empower people to make healthy changes in their lives. But people themselves must be willing to change.

Gary F. Gordon, cofounder of the American College for Advancement in Medicine, said, "I encourage people to learn to become their own doctors ... and realize we can learn something from everyone."

Characteristics of Good Healers

Part of being a health care practitioner is establishing a good relationship, or rapport, with a client. A good therapist will refer a client to another practitioner if this is not possible for some reason. In general, a client needs to be able to relax and feel safe with a therapist. The therapist needs to work on creating and maintaining this type of atmosphere.

The best healers are compassionate. This means they feel empathy for another person's situation in a nonjudgmental manner. In addition, healers must maintain a sense of detachment from their clients. A good healer must pay attention to his or her own health, and this includes not taking on other people's problems. Finding a balance between compassion and detachment can be challenging.

Good healers and health care practitioners address more than just the physical aspects of a person. They recognize the role that emotions, beliefs, and life circumstances can play in health and illness. While holistic approaches to health identify the locus, or place, of healing in the individual, it is important to recognize the role that factors beyond the control of the individual, such as poverty and prejudice, can have on health. It is also important to avoid blaming the victim. Making a person feel guilty by saying he or she caused the illness through a negative attitude or poor lifestyle choice is cruel. Such an approach is unlikely to help a person heal.

Our Planet, Ourselves

Hazel Parcell, an early alternative medicine proponent, influenced many alternative medicine pioneers, such as Bernard Jensen and Hannah Kruger. Parcell's work intimately connected people to the planet. She said it better than anyone: "Air, water and soil contamination lowers the life force of the planet and therefore of the human species. Since we are the earth, abuse of the planet's delicate ecosystems is tantamount to species suicide. A depressed planet produces depressed people . . . not only on the psychological level but the physical and spiritual realms as well. Physically we are most of the time only 'half-healthy' because the planetary life from which we draw our health has been compromised."

Holistic medicine reminds us that our bodies are creations of the natural world around us. To live healthy, we must live in harmony with the natural environment. For this reason we need to take care of the earth as if it is a natural extension of our bodies. Our individual bodies are microcosmic models of the planet.

In the early 1970s, two scientists, Lynn Margulis and James Lovelock, developed the Gaia theory. *Gaia* is ancient Greek for "earth." They proclaimed the earth is a living, breathing being. This idea is one most native religions had long ago. The earth has a respiratory system, the atmosphere; a circulatory system, the oceans and rivers; and a skeletal system, its landmasses. Humanity as a species constitute the self-reflecting nervous system interacting with the earth and the cosmos. Some histories claim that the Native American leader Chief Seattle knew this when in 1854 he was asked to sell his people's land to the federal government. His reply was, " . . . the earth does not belong to us. We belong to the earth. This we know: All things are connected like the blood which unites one family. . . Whatever we do to the earth we do to ourselves."

For some practitioners, any holistic approach to healing must include the very thing that has given us life, the earth. With organizations such as the Bioneers of the Collective Heritage Institute and Greenpeace International, we have a chance to revitalize ourselves and our planet.

Collective Heritage Institute
901 West San Mateo Road, Suite L
Santa Fe, NM 87505
(505) 986-0366
(877) 246-6337
Web site: http://www.bioneers.org

Greenpeace International
Keizersgracht 176
1016 DW Amsterdam
The Netherlands
+31 20 523 6222
e-mail: Services@ams.greenpeace.org
Web site: http://www.greenpeace.org

Part II
The Choices

The Primary Types of Alternative Therapies

The aim of all alternative therapies is to integrate the body, the mind, and the emotions. If any one element is off, a person will not be well. Each of the modalities discussed here attempts to do this in its own way. They differ widely in method, style, and degree.

Some treatments are hands-on, like the bodywork practices. Others, like homeopathy and Chinese medicine, involve a lengthy intake of questions that lead to a diagnosis. Still others treat acute and temporary problems by focusing on pain relief and structural matters, such as chiropractic and Rolfing. Most of the following therapies work by reducing stress, strengthening the body, and building a more powerful life force.

Whatever therapy you choose to perform, your job will be to encourage your patients to take a greater responsibility for their personal development, healing, and maintenance of health.

The various therapies outlined here may differ in their approaches, but they all are linked by a common philosophy:

1. They focus on empowering the individual to accept responsibility for at least part of his or her recovery and future health maintenance.
2. They emphasize a healthy diet and sound nutrition as the core of good health.
3. They recommend a balanced lifestyle, which includes exercise, rest, sleep, and emotional tranquility.
4. They attempt to ensure detoxification and the efficiency of the organs and systems of the body.
5. They recognize the importance of energy pathways (including the skeletal-muscular system, nerve centers, and meridians [energy movement linked to organs]) as potential sources of the body's internal physical and emotional health.
6. They treat the whole person, not just the symptoms.

This section is divided into three subcategories. Section A describes body-based therapies in which the patient is passive while the therapist performs the treatment. Section B describes practices that requires some kind of physical movement of the patient. Section C describes therapies that require the most education and often involve the patient ingesting a substance. Practitioners of these therapies need to have an in-depth understanding of the patient's medical history.

Section A: Body-Oriented Therapy

The therapies in this section all involve a hands-on approach to the body. The practitioner does the work by manipulating energy, soft tissue, or bones. Students need a certain sensitivity of touch and a level of awareness that lets them tune in directly to the body of the client. These are not necessarily intellectual modalities, although acupuncture, chiropractic, and osteopathy require years of theory and much diagnostic practice.

Acupuncture

The basis of all Chinese medicine is that there are energy pathways, or meridians, in the human body that connect the external surface of the body to the internal organs. Along these meridians are places where the life energy, or chi, naturally pools.

Essentially, acupuncture is the placement of needles along the meridians to either reduce an excess or tonify a deficiency connected to a particular internal organ. These organs also have emotional components as well. For instance, the kidneys hold fear, the liver holds anger, the heart holds overexcitement, the spleen and pancreas hold worry, and the lungs hold sadness. These organs are also related to the five elements of water, wood, fire, earth, and metal respectively. If a person is experiencing a particular emotion, treatment of the associated organ can help release the feelings.

A Session with an Acupuncturist

Acupuncture involves a long process of investigation, combining years of learned knowledge with intuitive insights. The most important step is discovering the root of the problem.

As soon as you enter an acupuncturist's office, the process of investigation begins. Everything that an acupuncturist notices is geared toward making an accurate diagnosis. Traditionally, Chinese medicine uses four ways to discover the underlying cause of a problem: looking, listening, asking, and feeling.

Looking: Chinese medicine holds that the only way to figure out what is happening on the inside is to observe what is manifested on the outside.

A good acupuncturist notices everything: your complexion, the quality of your hair and skin, the colors you are wearing, and most important, your vitality or spirit, which the Chinese call *shen*. How much shen you have will ultimately determine your ability to heal yourself. *The Yellow Emperor's Classic on Internal Medicine* states: "If there is spirit, the person thrives; if there is no spirit, the person dies."

Shen can be seen as the sparkle in the eyes, a healthy complexion, a harmonious state of mind, good deep breathing, and an enthusiasm for life. If a person lacks spirit, the complexion is dull, the muscles are withered, the eyes show no vitality, the mind is unclear, and the excitement for living is diminished.

Listening: As you sit down to discuss the reasons for your visit, the practitioner listens to the quality of your voice. He or she might also be aware of any particular odors that are present; every distinctive odor suggests a particular organ that might not be harmonious.

Asking: Prior to the first session, a patient is asked to complete an intake form, including the reasons for the visit, personal and family history, any past illnesses, and current signs and symptoms. The Chinese have devised ten questions to cover all areas of complaints from head to toe, as well as any problems that might exist in the circulatory, digestive, excretory, nervous, and respiratory systems.

Feeling: After the intake is evaluated, the acupuncturist will feel your pulse. This is one of the most difficult and skilled aspects of the whole educational process. To be a good pulse reader requires years of practice and a very subtle sensitivity.

In Western medicine, doctors are taught to find one pulse and measure its speed. In the Chinese tradition, speed is just one of a dozen qualities that can be detected. Also, there is not just one pulse; there are at least three on each wrist, each one having three levels, making a total of eighteen.

Practitioners are also taught to feel, or palpate, other areas of the body to get an understanding of the internal condition. In Japan, palpating (examination by touching) the abdomen is called *hara* diagnosis. The pathways, or the meridians, are also felt to detect obstructions that might affect the interior conditions.

After all of the above factors are evaluated, the acupuncturist seeks to understand the root of the current condition. He or she will assess if the patient's energy is some combination of excessive, exterior, and hot, or if it is deficient, internal, and cold. This technique is a part of a procedure called the eight principles of traditional Chinese medicine (TCM), which is taught in most of the acupuncture schools in the United States and in mainland China.

Five-element acupuncture is a method of acupuncture that tunes into more emotional causes of illness. It was part of the original Chinese concept of acupuncture, but it became emphasized in the West by J. R. Worsley. Worsley believes that in the past people were more affected by external conditions, but now the major problems stem from internal conditions, mental and emotional. The five-element system focuses on the connections between organs and emotions.

After a diagnosis is made in either the five-element or the TCM approach, a treatment plan is devised and acupuncture needles are placed on points along the meridians. The needles balance and harmonize the internal organs. Acupuncture requires knowing the energetic activity of each point and the way to manipulate the needles to affect the interior balance.

The curriculum of most acupuncture schools includes Chinese medical theory and diagnosis, differentiation of syndromes (how different exterior and interior conditions affect the body), meridian and point energetics, needle technique, and treatment of disease. There are also specialized courses in the use of five-element theory, auricular acupuncture, scalp acupuncture, treatment of sports injuries, and the use of electronic applications.

Most schools also offer an intense program in Chinese herbology that either supplements the acupuncture treatments or can be used as the sole source of treatment. Historically, acupuncture and herbology stem from separate traditions. Much of the theory learned in schools can be applied to either healing modality. The value of learning both is that some people respond better to acupuncture and others to herbs.

The Growth of Acupuncture

The Food and Drug Administration's (FDA) sanctioning of acupuncture needles as medical devices has made the technique more acceptable. This has opened the door for some doctors to recommend acupuncture for situations that they do not know how to treat—not just chronic pain and arthritis, but internal medical situations such as an under-functioning liver or kidney. With this growth comes reimbursement from insurance agencies. Companies like Oxford and Blue Cross have special plans that accept acupuncture and other certified therapics, but only with practitioners that have been approved by these companies.

Schools

Most acupuncture schools are three- to four-year programs, and tuition begins at $5,000 a year. If you need financial assistance, you may wish to attend a college accredited by the Accreditation Commission for Acupuncture and Oriental Medicine (ACAOM). ACAOM is recognized by the U.S. Department of Education, and students enrolled in accredited programs may be eligible for federal student loans. Schools are usually three- to four-year programs, which qualify you to take the

National Certification Commission for Acupuncture and Oriental Medicine (NCCAOM) exam.

Many acupuncture schools do not require candidates to have an undergraduate degree. However, all accredited schools require at least two years of undergraduate study, such as community college, prior to entry. Many state that they prefer applicants to have a bachelor's degree. The biological sciences are good preparation for the field. Most schools offer full-time programs, but some have part-time programs. A 1993 survey by the California Acupuncture Association showed practitioners' gross annual income ranged from $30,000 to more than $100,000 per year.

See the For More Information section of this book for a listing of schools, or for more information, contact the NCCAOM:

> National Certification Commission
>   for Acupuncture and Oriental
>   Medicine (NCCAOM)
> 11 Canal Center Plaza, Suite 300
> Alexandria, VA 22314
> (703) 548-9004
> Web site: http://www.nccaom.org

Bodywork

The term "bodywork" refers to all hands-on techniques—manipulating the body for therapeutic purposes. The foundation of all bodywork is massage. Therapies like Rolfing and Trager are derivatives of massage. Most bodywork usually does not include a diagnosis of illness, although therapies like shiatsu and reflexology aim to detect physical imbalances.

Bodywork is generally not covered by insurance companies. Only massage has state licensure. Most other therapies have their own certifications that are not state or nationally recognized.

History of Massage

Rubbing the body when it is sore or bruised is an automatic response of almost every human being. Therapeutic touch is assumed to have developed from an oral tradition of folk medicine. The ancient Chinese book *The Cong-Fou of the Tao-Tse*, which appeared in French more than 100 years ago, presents an elaborate system of bodywork. This book is probably the foundation of both our modern massage and of the Swedish massage techniques.

Some 8,000 years ago, the Yoga cult in India used respiratory exercises for religious and healing purposes, as recorded in its ancient doctrines of wisdom, the Vedas. Egyptian, Persian, and old Japanese medical texts are full of references to bath and massage treatments for various ailments.

In 430 BC Hippocrates wrote, "It is necessary to rub the shoulder following reduction of a dislocated shoulder." Asclepius, another Greek physician in the tradition of Hippocrates, relied exclusively on the art and practice of massage. He claimed that stroking the body effected a cure by restoring natural, free movement to nutritive fluids. He also discovered that gently touching the body could induce a patient to relax and sleep. The Romans also used massage techniques as a major part of their healing practices.

Between the 1850s and the early 1900s, massage was practiced in the spas of Germany, Austria, and France. People suffering from rheumatism made yearly trips to health spas to take the "cure," which consisted of exercise and therapeutic massage, the consumption of mineral water, and the taking of hot mineral baths.

The trend toward holistic health care in the United States has brought a demand for therapeutic massage. It is an important aspect of the self-care philosophy of keeping the body well through exercise, nutrition, relaxation, and stress reduction.

Therapeutic Purpose

The purpose of massage or bodywork is to bring about physiological, mechanical, or psychological healing. It does this by relaxing the body, relieving pain, reducing accumulated water in the body (edema), and increasing the range of motion of the muscles. It helps immensely in the treatment of injured or ill people. It can also prepare muscles for strenuous activity or help muscles recover from such activity.

Emotional Effects

Touching the body with the intention of effecting a positive change is a healing art. It is a way to show caring. It is also a unique way of communicating without words. Anthropologist and writer Ashley Montagu, in his book *Touching*, explains how a soothing touch is essential to life. Montagu points out that newborn animals must be licked by their mothers if they are to survive, and that rats that are petted grow and learn faster and develop greater immunity to disease than those that are not. Research has shown that infants who are deprived of touch develop abnormal physical and emotional symptoms.

Touch is also a way we share our energy with another person. Thomas Claire, author of *Bodywork: What Type of Massage to Get and How to Make the Most of It*, writes: "Bodywork and massage, in my opinion, help us to be more creative and more alert. Bodywork helps us connect with our inner center, and with our inner resources, which is a very hard thing to do today. I believe that touch is a vital aspect of health, and the more our society becomes high-tech, the more we need high touch. It is estimated that 80 percent of all illnesses are triggered by stress. Massage and bodywork induce relaxation and can help us maintain health and ward off disease."

Physiological Effects

Bodywork therapies work on the physical level with the soft tissue of the body—muscles, tendons, ligaments, and sometimes internal organs. Massage or bodywork can bring about a balance of the metabolic processes within the soft tissue. It does this by assisting the flow of blood through the veins, encouraging lymphatic drainage, stretching tissues that can tend to be tight and contracted, and relieving the interfering presence of subcutaneous (beneath the skin) scar tissue. Also, the stimulation of the sensory receptors of the skin and subcutaneous tissue causes increased reflex responses.

This in turn, leads to a greater capacity to respond to internal and external environmental signals.

Choosing a Bodywork Practice

To choose a type of bodywork practice, it is helpful to look at the principles behind each modality. All of the therapies discussed below use tactile skills of touch with fingers and hands, but they involve different levels of sensitivity and depth of pressure. Some bodywork practices emphasize the physical; whereas others are more mental, emotional, or spiritual in approach. Some, like Swedish massage, use strictly physical sensation and practical techniques. Others involve oral communication and the increasing awareness of the client's mind-body relationship. Reiki, polarity, and therapeutic touch involve more energy work than physical action. Ideally, any bodywork therapist should be familiar with many techniques and approaches to health.

Massage

Modern use of massage as a therapeutic modality in the West began in Sweden with Henrik Ling (1776-1839). A fencing master and gymnastics instructor, Ling began to investigate massage after he had cured himself of rheumatism in the arm by means of percussion (use of pressure and release). He developed the simultaneous application of massage and medical gymnastics because he saw massage as a form of passive gymnastics. At the time Ling was developing his techniques, anatomy and physiology were gaining acceptance, and provided a scientific framework for his theories. Ling's methods became known as the Swedish Movement Treatment. In 1813, the Royal Gymnastic Central Institute became the first college to include massage in its curriculum. Through the publication of Ling's ideas, his system became the basis of standard massage practice. The profession of physical therapy also developed out of these techniques.

Massage is very useful in the relief of muscle tension. Muscles become tense from overuse and can become tight. If a muscle stays tense long enough without any relief or relaxation, then pain, stiffness, and even inflammation can occur. If this condition becomes chronic, the muscle will become less elastic and more fibrous, placing increased stress where it is anchored to the bone. If this happens along the back, the tense muscles can cause structural problems, throwing the vertebrae and discs out of alignment. This creates additional problems of increased pain, coordination difficulties, and stress on the joints. Left untreated, the muscle eventually enters the exhaustion stage, where fibrous tissue and inflammation degenerate into fibrosis, and the joints can develop arthritis due to the extra stress.

Massage can help at any level of this process, but it is most beneficial in the early stage. Essentially, massage allows blood to flow back into the muscle. When a muscle is tense it is like a knot, and no fluid or nutrients and very little blood can flow in to nourish that part of the body, which is essential to maintain overall health.

Ten Principles of a Great Massage

1. Be centered and focused.
2. Respect the recipient fully: Have clear intention.

3. Listen to the client's body and breath with your hands, heart, ears, and intuition.
4. Massage to create more space (length and breadth) and breathing room.
5. Massage to facilitate movement. Include secure range of motion work.
6. Massage toward the heart to improve blood circulation and lymph return.
7. Massage muscles thoroughly: body, tendons, insertions.
8. Start gently, then massage deeper.
9. Massage as deep as is comfortable for the client. Listen very carefully to the recipient's body and breath.
10. Cool down after deep work. Don't over-massage an area.

There are more than 50,000 massage therapists practicing in the United States. To obtain a license, most states require 250 to 2,200 hours of classroom and hands-on study. Check with the Commission on Massage Training for state-by-state requirements.

Curriculum: Most schools have required courses in shiatsu, polarity, aromatherapy, sports massage, and others.

Tuition: Costs for professional programs range from $2,000 to $10,000 per year. Financial aid is available for accredited schools.

Earnings: Spas, health clubs, and resorts are constantly seeking qualified massage therapists. Most of these companies may charge $150 for a massage and pay the therapist half of this. Many therapists build a clientele at these clubs, and then expand into their own businesses. With good recommendations, a massage therapist can earn over $50,000 per year.

For more information, contact:

Commission on Massage Training
   Approval/Accreditation (COMTAA)
c/o American Massage Therapy Association
820 Davis Street, Suite 100
Evanston, IL 60201-4444
(847) 864-0123
Web site: http://www.amtamassage.org

Rolfing (Structional Integration)

The Rolf Institute was founded in 1972 by Ida P. Rolf, Ph.D. Rolf claimed that painful emotions, illnesses, surgery, and other traumas result in compression and distortion of the body. These events are physically held within us until they can be released.

Rolfing differs from other body therapies because it reaches very deep to release adhesions of the fascia (connecting body tissues). Like all holistic therapies, Rolfing is not the means of healing, but the means of removing the obstacles that allow the body to heal itself. Ida Rolf said, "When the body gets working appropriately the force of gravity can flow through. Then, spontaneously, the body heals itself."

Cost: Students can expect the Rolfing training program to last one to two years and cost between $11,200 and $13,500.

Requirements: Before studying Rolfing, students must have an understanding of therapeutic touch, anatomy, kinesiology, and physiology. Those with academic foundations in bodywork are not required to take this course. However, many students with extensive backgrounds find the unique Rolfing perspective of the class worthwhile.

Treatment: Each session lasts about one and a half hours and practitioners are usually required to treat the whole body. Most Rolfers charge between $100 to $150 per session.

For more information, contact:

> The Rolf Institute of Structural Integration
> 205 Canyon Boulevard
> Boulder, CO 80302
> (800) 530-8875
> (303) 449-5903
> e-mail: rolfinst@aol.com
> Web site: http://www.rolf.org

Chiropractic

Chiropractic is the second largest primary health care field in the world. It is licensed in all fifty states and is practiced by more than 50,000 people in over fifty countries. More than 15 million people per year see chiropractors. Total enrollment in United States chiropractic colleges in the fall of 1995 was 14,040. The mean enrollment per college was 878. Between 1990 and 1995 enrollment increased by 44 percent. A profile of chiropractic students found that they were most attracted to the profession because of its holistic, drugless, and natural approach to health.

History

It all began one day in 1895. Daniel David Palmer, a grocer and part-time spiritual healer, was asked to work on a man who had been deaf for seventeen years. In his biography, Palmer describes the sudden onset of the man's condition: "When he was exerting himself in a cramped and stooped position, he felt something give way in his back and immediately became deaf." Upon examining the man, Palmer found a subluxation (a misaligned vertebra) along the spine. Palmer had the man lie on his stomach and applied firm pressure to his spine with his hands. The vertebra was realigned, and suddenly the man could hear again.

From this and other remarkable cures, Palmer concluded that "a sublexed vertebra is the cause of ninety-five percent of all diseases." Based on this theory, he developed a systematic and scientific method of adjusting the spinal vertebrae. A local minister proposed the name "chiropractic" from the Greek root *chiro* meaning "done by hand." Before the end of 1895, he opened a school of chiropractic in Davenport, Iowa.

Palmer believed that people have two types of intelligence: innate and educated. "Innate retains its education acquired in past ages. Educated starts in life without any knowledge of the past." He believed that innate intelligence is activated by adjusting the spine; once nerve interference is removed, this innate intelligence is able to take over and healing can occur. Palmer also concluded that human beings are diseased only when the mind fails to perform its function. To him, the mind governed all organic functions through connections with the nerves of the body. He stated: "The brain impulse is generated by the brain under the command of the innate mind or the soul and is carried along nerves to every individual cell in the living organism, regulating its function." He also spoke of chiropractic in relation to more expansive spiritual concepts, such as self-healing, vitalism, life energy, and harmony.

Palmer's son, B. J. Palmer, made chiropractic a success and promoted it nationally. Today, the majority of chiropractors concentrate on the structural support of the nervous system along the spine. The range of treatment involves much more than adjustments and can include nutritional consultations, massage, and applied kinesiology.

Schools

Currently, all sixteen chiropractic schools in the United States have accredited status from the Council on Chiropractic Education (CCE). A minimum of two years of undergraduate education are required with successful completion of courses with a grade of "C" or better in biology, general chemistry, organic chemistry, physics, psychology, english/communication, and the humanities. Most chiropractic programs consist of four academic years of professional education averaging a total of approximately 4,800 hours.

For more information on chiropractic schools, contact:

World Chiropractic Alliance
2950 North Dobson Road, Suite 1
Chandler, AZ 85224
(800) 347-1011
Web site: http://www.
    worldchiropracticalliance.org

Osteopathy

Osteopathy, which means "bone treatment," was originally a holistic approach to aligning the body. It was developed in the nineteenth century by Andrew Taylor Still. Still was a renegade physician who believed healing was an innate tendency of the body. He refused to use drugs on his patients and developed a new system of treatment utilizing the manipulation of various joints and tissues of the body to reduce structural interference. The manipulations in osteopathy are essentially the same as those of chiropractic, but chiropractors restrict their work to the spine whereas osteopaths work on all joints

Osteopaths believe that disruption of the nerve flow, from a muscle spasm at the root of the nerve or from injury or illness, is the cause of disease. Health depends on uninterrupted nerve flow from the brain and spinal cord through the skin and associated tissues to the organs. Still discovered that his treatments were helpful for aches and pains as well as for bacterial infections.

When Still was asked what he would prescribe in place of drugs, he replied, "We can give you an adjustment of structure but we cannot give you anything from the material world that would be beneficial to the workings of a perfect machine. A perfectly adjusted body will produce pure blood and plenty of it, deliver it on time and in quantity sufficient to supply all demands in the economy of life. This is what the osteopath can give you in the place of drugs if he knows his business."

Although the osteopathic profession started out with more hands-on therapy, most contemporary osteopathic physicians' practices are nearly identical to regular medical providers'. Essentially osteopaths are considered doctors. They are primary health care providers for millions of people. Like medical doctors, they must meet the necessary education and licensure requirements to practice medicine. They are also the only other professionals who can legally perform surgery and prescribe medication.

Schools

To be considered for admission to one of the osteopathic medical schools, applicants typically complete four years of undergraduate work, culminating in a bachelor's degree. Most osteopathic medical schools also require one year of English, biological sciences, physics, general chemistry, and organic chemistry. Some schools have other requirements, such as genetics, mathematics, or psychology. These requirements are listed in the catalogs available from each osteopathic medical school.

Applicants should take the Medical College Admissions Test (MCAT) during their junior year of college. The MCAT examines knowledge and skills in areas such as biology, math, reading, and problem solving. A premed adviser can assist applicants in scheduling and preparing for this examination.

Most future doctors of osteopathy (D.O.s) major in sciences such as biology or chemistry in their undergraduate studies. However, applicants may major in any area as long as they meet the minimum course and grade requirements, and demonstrate their potential for successfully completing an osteopathic medical curriculum.

Prospective osteopathic medical students must also exhibit a genuine concern for people. Osteopathic medicine is a people-oriented profession that demands dedicated and empathetic individuals. Osteopathic colleges require a personal interview to assess the applicant's communication skills and learn more about why that person wants to become an osteopathic physician. The applicant may wish to spend some time with a D.O., or do volunteer work in health care before applying.

Requirements: Four years of undergraduate studies are required. Most students major in sciences, but other areas are acceptable if you meet the requirements of the school. Training in osteopathic medical schools requires a concentration in physical diagnosis and evaluation.

For more information about Osteopathy, contact the American Osteopathic Association.

American Osteopathic Association (AOA)

The AOA is a national professional association of osteopaths. The AOA accredits the colleges of osteopathic medicine, osteopathic internships and residency programs, and health care facilities. The AOA's Web site offers general information on osteopathic medicine (http://www.am-osteo-assn.org).

Section B: Kinesthetic (Movement) Therapies

The therapies described in this section are based on the belief that healing capacities are inherent in directly cultivating, sensing, and experiencing one's body. The developers of the following modalities believed that sacred wisdom lay in the body's natural expression. They felt that having the body find its most comfortable axis of movement would help free up blockages.

These therapies differ in many areas, but they share the common assumption that sensing, feeling, moving, breathing, and changing posture are crucial in the individual's search for health. The therapies are hands-on but they also involve the participation of the client in moving or posturing in a particular way.

Alexander Technique (AT)

Developed by Frederick Matthias Alexander, a self-taught therapist and actor, this technique is a way of educating the body to act in its most efficient manner. If the postures and movements we perform are done according to proper structural alignment, we use the least amount of energy and our body has less internal stress.

Practitioners are called teachers because they teach people how to use the mind in conjunction with the body to identify and change poor and inefficient habits of moving and being. With simple oral commands and clear hands-on guidance, the body is introduced to a different way of organizing and initiating movement.

The feature that makes the Alexander Technique different from other alignment coordination therapies is that it focuses on naturally lengthening the spine to create an upward and freeing extension of the neck. Patients claim that the results are a feeling of floating up and forward in the world and a lengthening and widening of the back.

In an Alexander Technique session, your teacher observes how you move and helps you understand how your movement style relates to your symptom. With a "words-and-touch" approach, you are instructed to move differently. Using a unique hands-on method to elicit your primary control, the instructor gives you an experience of dynamic expansion. With this, you learn how to replicate that expansion on your own. This powerful shift gives your body a highly responsive coordination. This gentle, supportive touch helps you notice tension and allows you to experience your body in a ncw way.

Controlled studies have shown that AT is very useful in dealing with back pain, helping the elderly to balance while walking, and improving breathing functions. In addition, AT has been shown to help in combating the disability and depression of Parkinson's disease. For full benefit, a recommended course is thirty private sessions, at an average time of thirty to forty-five minutes per session. Rates vary from $60 to $100 per session.

Schools: 1,600 hours of class instruction over three years are required. Classes usually have a five-to-one student/teacher ratio.

Certification: Call the North American Society of

Teachers of the Alexander Technique (NASTAT) for approved teacher training courses in your area.

For more information, contact:

North American Society of Teachers of the
    Alexander Technique (NASTAT)
3010 Hennepin Avenue South, Suite 10
Minneapolis, MN 55408
(800) 473-0620
e-mail: nastat@ix.netcom.com

Feldenkrais Method (Functional Integration)

The Feldenkrais Method is a body-centered process developed by Israeli physics engineer and judo expert Dr. Moshe Feldenkrais around 1949. The method is considered a learning technique, not a therapy or way of healing. Dr. Feldenkrais's idea was to become aware of all of one's movements. Even the simplest movement, like holding a pen or lifting your arm, involves a thousand subtle movements.

Two techniques are used to communicate the work. The first and original way, Functional Integration, involves a hands-on, gentle manipulation exchange between practitioner and client to show the body a more effective way of moving. Awareness Through Movement, the other technique, is designed for group purposes. Clients are guided through a sequence of movements called lessons. Participants are not taught to perform movement; they are taught to experiment with their bodies. Students learn that there are no right or wrong ways of doing things; there is only the individual's way.

The Feldenkrais Method uses four main principles: ease of movement, absence of resistance, presence of reversibility, and comfortable breathing. In his book, *The Potent Self, A Guide to Spontaneity*, Feldenkrais suggests: "In good action, the sensation of effort is absent, no matter what the actual expenditure of energy is." He adds: "The mature person clears up all irrelevant motivations and uses interest, necessity, and skill unhindered by unrecognized emotional urges."

The recognition of resistance, emotional or physical, is very important in the Feldenkrais Method. Reversibility means the ability, inherent in all of us, to change things in our lives that do not work with ease. Comfortable breathing is part of this ease in living. Many people hold their breath constantly because of unconscious inhibitions. This holding affects the body image and forces them to continuously rearrange their throat, chest, and abdomen before they can even speak.

Another tenet of the Feldenkrais Method is that, given the encounters and challenges you have faced in the past, you have the ideal body for coping with the stresses you face. A Feldenkrais practitioner does not look at pain, poor posture, or limited movement as symptoms of something being wrong; instead, he or she sees these as the best possible choices that the physical-emotional body could make at the time, given the perception of the choices you had. The practitioner's job is to increase your perception by showing you what is possible for the body and thus increasing your choices and ways of being in the world.

Many physically challenged people use Feldenkrais to expand their range of coordination. It is also being incorporated by many physical therapists as part of their formal schooling. A minimum of 800 hours and over 160 days of training are required, which can be accomplished between thirty-six and forty-eight months.

For more information, contact:

Feldenkrais Resources
830 Bancroft Way, Suite 112
Berkeley, CA 94710
(800) 765-1907
(510) 540-7600
e-mail: feldenres@aol.com
Web site: http://www.feldenkrais-resources.com

Pilates

The hottest new holistic movement therapy has been around for over seventy years. The Pilates method has been popular with dancers since the 1940s, but today followers range from athletes, physiotherapists, and fitness trainers to health care providers and other professionals who appreciate the significant role exercise plays in restoring and maintaining good health. Recently, it has generated so much enthusiasm that Pilates equipment and instructors are on hand in many fitness centers around the country. Like Feldenkrais and Alexander, Pilates has its own original ideas about moving the body in the most optimal way.

The originator, Joseph H. Pilates, was born in Germany in 1880. He developed this fitness regime and successfully used it to overcome his disabilities as a frail and sickly child. Pilates uses a set of exercises to developed and strengthen the "core area" of the body—abdominals, lower back, buttocks, and upper thighs. The patients performs a series of controlled movements that engage the mind and body. The lithe musculature and ease of movement possessed by a cat is an image Pilates used to illustrate the technique's objectives.

Emphasis is placed on developing deep torso strength and flexibility, known as centering, to ensure proper posture and reduced risk of injury. The Pilates method places a lot of emphasis on correct posture and technique, and doesn't rely on high numbers of repetitive exercises.

Many participants feel Pilates creates body awareness. There is a Pilates stance—lying on the floor, everything touching evenly, and the stomach tightened by sinking the navel to the spine—which is important to the proper execution of the exercises.

Unlike the Feldenkrais Method and the Alexander Technique, which use only the body, Pilates is performed alternately on floor mats and on a device called a universal reformer, a spring-controlled bedlike frame. This is used to properly support and align the body in a variety of fluid movements, coupled with gentle resistance. Most exercises involve the resistance of the body itself.

Pilates sessions range from $60 to $80 and a number of them are recommended per week to help the body gain flexibility.

Courses: Courses are usually offered three times per year, for three months and require a commitment of fifteen to twenty hours per week.

Cost: $1,125 for one course and up to $2,250 for three courses.

For more information about training, contact:

Stott Pilates International Certification Center
2200 Yonge Street, Suite 1402
Toronto, ON M4S 2C2

Canada
(800) 910-0001
e-mail: education@stottpilates.com
Web site: http://www.stottpilates.com

Section C: Internal Therapies

The therapies in this section differ from those in the two previous sections because they depend on some form of internal application. Oral therapy is vital to these modalities. All are based on systems of medicine that require years of schooling. They rely on thorough investigation of the underlying causes of illness in the body. These modalities of treatment also depend on intellectual thought and diagnostic study of underlying conditions. Major principles are the prevention of disease and the importance of early detection.

Ayurvedic Studies

Ayurveda, pronounced "Aa-your-vay-da," means the "science of life." *Ayur* means "life" and *veda* means "knowledge." It originated in India more than 10,000 years ago and is believed to be the oldest healing science in existence, from which all other systems emerged. Ayurveda theory evolved from a deep understanding of creation. The great *rishis*, or seers, of ancient India came to understand creation through deep meditation and other spiritual practices. The rishis sought to reveal the deepest truths of human physiology and health. They observed the fundamentals of life, organized them into an elaborate system, and compiled India's philosophical and spiritual texts, called Veda.

Five thousand years ago in India, a medical system around Ayurveda was developed that is still practiced today. It uses herbal tonics, massage, dietary changes, food therapy, exercise, yoga, meditation, special baths, medicated inhalations, and prayers sung in Sanskrit, the language of the ancient Hindus.

Deepak Chopra, M.D., an endocrinologist who has recently popularized Ayurvedic medicine, says that the first thing an Ayurvedic physician asks is, "Who is my patient?" By "who" the physician does not mean your name, but how you are constituted. Constitution, the key to this system, refers to the overall health profile of the person, including strengths and susceptibilities. Understanding the subtle intricacies of a person's constitution is the first critical step in understanding the person.

According to Ayurveda, every human being is a creation of the cosmos, and everything in the universe (people, food, animals, nature and diseases) are combinations of three energy-elements: air (called *Vayu* or *Vata*), fire (called *Pitta*), and water (called *Kapha*). When these elements are balanced, one is healthy. Illness is defined as an imbalance of these elements; all disorders are excesses of one or more elements.

A person's constitution *(dosha)* is predominantly one or more of these elements. Each element relates to certain body types, foods, and health concerns. By nature, whatever a person's constitution is, it has a tendency to become excessed. For example, a person with an air constitution (Vayu dosha) is thin and bony.

Physical symptoms of excess air include dry skin, cracking bones, gas, and constipation. Mental symptoms of excess air include fear, worry, anxiety, and nervousness. When a Vayu dosha person is balanced, he or she is creative and adaptable and has no physical health concerns. Ayurveda notes that certain foods increase air and other foods reduce air. In general, excess air is reduced by eating cooked or steamed foods, and eating every three or four hours. Foods like carrots, rice, and mung beans reduce excess air. Broccoli, baked beans and barley increase air (for example, they cause gas). Excessive lifestyles also increase the air element.

People with fire constitution (Pitta dosha) tend toward excess heat. When healthy, they are strong, make good leaders, and are warm and goal oriented. When the Pitta dosha is imbalanced, they become hot tempered, impatient, and irritable. Physically, they develop heat-related disorders such as acne, rashes, diarrhea, ulcers, toxic blood, and liver, kidney, gall bladder, heart and spleen disorders. Water constitutions (Kapha doshas) tend toward excess water. When healthy they are strong, muscular, calm, and loyal. When water becomes excessed, they develop lethargy, and a hoarding or greedy nature. Physically, they develop conditions such as congestion, edema, and heart and kidney problems, or they become overweight.

The dosha is the blueprint that outlines all innate tendencies of a person's system. One's dosha and the characteristics that reveal it can clarify why one person has a negative reaction to milk, chili, loud noise, or humidity, while another person can easily tolerate these things. Each body type responds differently to many things and flourishes on a specific diet, exercise plan, and lifestyle.

Ayurvedic medicine holds that seven major factors influence the equilibrium of the doshas: genetics, internal trauma, external trauma, natural tendencies, seasonal tendencies, habits, and magnetic and electrical influences. According to Virender Sodhi, M.D., director of the American School of Ayurvedic Sciences in Bellevue, Washington: "Disease is the result of the disruption of the spontaneous flow of nature's intelligence within our physiology."

Ayurveda holds that health is the soundness and balance between body, mind, and spirit, and the equilibrium of the doshas. This ancient healing system has three main focuses: healing illness, prevention of disease, and longevity or age reversal.

Public awareness of Ayurveda is now close to where chiropractic was forty years ago and where acupuncture was around twenty years ago. However, Ayurveda is continually gaining recognition as a very effective form of treatment. Despite the requirement of extensive training, no national or state licensure is available. Many educational programs are short; others are full-time and in depth.

Chinese Medicine

Chinese medicine is the world's oldest continuously practiced medicine. Over one-quarter of the population of the world uses some form of it. Chinese medicine as it is mostly practiced in mainland China and in the United States today is called traditional Chinese medicine (TCM). The basic principles of TCM are outlined in the section on acupuncture. The name "traditional" is not really accurate. Chinese medicine has traditional elements, but it is really a conglomerate of many different approaches that were codified in the middle of the twentieth century by Mao Tse Tung and the Communist Party, and called TCM. Because of the communist belief in atheism, much of the Taoist spiritual nature of the true tradition is not taught.

Taoism is the root of Chinese medicine. *Tao* means "the way" or "the path." It is the spiritual understanding of the harmonious flow of the cosmos and universal life energies. It is the foundation of the teaching of the legendary Yellow Emperor, the founder of classical Chinese medicine and culture.

The Yellow Emperor was taught by his court physician that in the internal and external life of the human being, there are cycles related to the times of the day and the seasons. According to classical Chinese medicine, there is a natural flow of energy or *qi (chi)* that alternates its flow in rhythmic harmony; sometimes passive, sometimes aggressive. These energies make up everything in the universe and the Chinese call them *yin* and *yang*. The yang energy is male, light, and positive, while the yin forces are feminine, dark, and negative. Everything has a yin and yang element to it; you can not have one without the other.

In the West, we think these forces are opposites, but in the East they are seen as complementary and one gives rise to the other, the way day gives rise to night. Together they form the whole.

This is the symbol for yin and yang developed in China ages ago.

Our bodies also have a yin and yang aspect to them. The front is yin and the back is yang. The outside is yang and the inside is yin. The upper moving parts floating toward heaven are yang and the lower parts sinking to the earth are yin.

In ancient times, understanding the Tao was the basis of the ten-year study of Chinese medicine that included expertise in the following areas.

Acupuncture became the basis for all forms of healing in the Chinese system, because it mapped out the energy pathways or meridian system. Classical acupuncture is based on the five elements of the Tao: water, wood, fire, earth, and metal and their relationships to the internal organs.

Chinese herbology relies on the meridians, tastes, and energetics of plants such as hot, cold, dry, or damp, for their healing abilities.

Chinese therapeutic massage is also a specific field of study today called Tui Na. Tui means "to push" and na means "to grasp." It has also been referred to as amma therapy (am is "to press" and ma is "to touch"). There is also nien ("to pinch"), char ("to scrub"), and seven other techniques making a total of thirteen different therapeutic ways of doing this type of practice. Treatments aim at balancing, restoring, and promoting optimum health. This tradition also has the ability to set bones.

Moxabustion is the burning of herbs, usually artemesia or mugwort above an acupuncture point to help infuse it with energy. This practice is now used along with acupuncture and is taught as an important part of the curriculum in all acupuncture schools.

Feng Shui or **Geomancy** has become extremely popular in the last few years. A more detailed explanation is given in the next chapter.

Astrology was an important part of the ancient Chinese medical program. If the individual is a microcosm of the universe, then watching natural cycles and knowing when to perform certain treatments could have a greater effect on the person.

Diet and the **energetics of food** are crucial to Chinese medicine. The five tastes are used to have different effects on the body. Sweet for tonifying organs particularly the spleen, sour for the liver, salty for pulling the energy into the kidneys, bitter for pulling the energy into and helping the heart, and pungent for opening and tonifying the lungs.

Qigong is known as an internal martial art. It is a series of exercises that promotes the flow of healing energy. Hundreds of different exercises have been developed throughout the centuries for different types of healing. Schools generally do not teach acupuncture or herbology but mainly concentrate on teaching Taoist practices of energy movement.

Herbology

Herbs are the medicines of the earth. They were the first medicines for all cultures and all civilizations.

Historians have said that humanity and the plant kingdom share a symbiotic relationship. As plants have been cultivated, they have furthered our growth with medicines and food sources. We have propagated and evolved plants, adding to the diversity and to the evolution of different species.

Pharmaceutical drugs have taken from herbs the active ingredients found to be the most effective. They do not include the other substances of the plant, which also may serve an important function. Herbologists believe that the nonactive substances of the plant are needed to create a synergistic effect of the healing substances as well as to minimize the side effects of the main ingredient. Synergy means that the combination is more effective than single ingredients.

Herbology is a powerful healing modality. Echinacea and goldenseal root are two herbs that are becoming very popular as natural antibiotics. In the Chinese tradition, white peony and angelica *(dang kwei)* have long been used to regulate menstruation. Other herbs are used as preventatives. Stinging nettle tea is used to purify the blood and gives energy. Ginseng has always been popular for increasing vitality. This does not mean that all herbs are safe. Some may have side effects and it is important to be careful. Even though herbs are natural, they can still have dangerous chemical constituents.

While most herbs can be ingested in the form of teas, there is a great assortment of ways to prepare herbal medicine that all students of herbology must learn.

Tinctures are alcohol-based solutions of single or combined herbs that are soaked for a certain length of time—a process that pulls out the vital chemical constituents of the herb. Tinctures are very powerful and are taken orally.

Infusions are teas made by pouring hot water over fresh or dried herbs. Boiling is not recommended for leaves and flowers because it can destroy some of the important chemical ingredients that emerge slowly with the addition of hot water. Usually this brew is left to stand for ten to twenty minutes and then strained and drunk. Some people make a sun tea, where herbs are left in a jar in the sun for a day and drunk with the same overall benefit as an infusion.

Decoctions are similar to infusions, but the herbs are boiled and then left to simmer. In this process, the leaves, flowers, roots, and even the bark are used. Many Chinese herbal formulas are made this way.

Poultices are mashed or powdered herbs that are applied directly to the skin to reduce inflammations or draw out toxins. Sometimes cheesecloth is placed around the herbs to hold them in place. Substances like daikon leaves and fresh grated ginger root are very beneficial for lung infections.

Compresses use boiled herbs that are applied to the skin like a poultice.

Salves use boiled herbs and a mixture of vegetable oil or beeswax and are applied to injuries or external infections.

Ointments are similar to salves but the mixtures are made with petroleum-based products.

In the United States, Native American reservations are the only places where physicians can legally diagnose and prescribe herbal remedies.

Certification: There are no accreditation or nationally recognized certification programs in herbology, except for those pertaining to Chinese herbs. The National Board for the Certification of Acupuncturists has recently formed another organization for certification in Chinese herbs. However, there is no overall association that regulates or accredits education in herbal medicine. Prospective students should examine the use of herbs in many different traditions, both Eastern and Western, to see what they feel most comfortable with.

Schools: Most schools do not have any prerequisites, but a background in botany is useful.

Holistic Health Practitioner

A holistic health practitioner is someone who has combined many different treatment modalities into a whole approach to working with people. Many people who have studied different therapies and who have combined therapies like massage, nutrition, herbology, and polarity into a unique practice call themselves holistic health therapists.

There are a growing number of schools that give students a general survey of holistic medicine. These schools offer courses ranging from Chinese medicine principles and basic massage techniques to polarity and shamanic initiation. One such school is the Academy of Natural Healing, which offers a unique intern program for high school students who are willing to volunteer time around the school in exchange for classes and hands-on practice.

These schools offer programs that can last from months to years. None of these schools are accredited except those that offer a master's degree in counseling. For those interested in advanced studies in holistic medicine, naturopathy may be a good field to explore. Naturopathic physicians (NDs) are licensed professionals who have completed over 4,400 hours of required study.

Naturopathy or Naturopathic Medicine

Naturopathic medicine, sometimes called naturopathy, is as old as healing itself and as new as the latest discoveries in biochemical sciences. The earliest doctors and healers worked with herbs, foods, water, fasting, and tissue manipulation—gentle treatments that do not obscure the body's own healing powers. Today's naturopathic physicians continue to use these therapies as their main tools and to advocate a healthy dose of primary prevention. In addition, modern naturopathic doctors (NDs) conduct and make practical use of the latest biochemical research involving nutrition, botanicals, homeopathy, and other natural treatments. Naturopathic medicine is a distinct system of primary health care—an art, science, philosophy, and practice of diagnosing, treating, and preventing disease. Naturopathic medicine's techniques include modern, traditional, scientific, and empirical methods.

The Science of Naturopathic Medicine

The science of naturopathic medicine is an ever-expanding body of knowledge drawn from diverse traditional and modern sources. The practice is said to be the true continuation of the Hippocratic tradition, and its first principle is Hippocrates' mandate, "Do no harm."

Illness is not caused simply by an invasion of external agents or germs, but it is a manifestation of the organism's attempt to defend and heal itself. The physician's role is to identify and remove agents blocking the healing process, bolster the patient's healing capacity, and support the creation of a healthy internal and external environment.

The body has the inherent ability—the vitality—not only to heal itself and restore health, but also to ward off disease. Illness does not occur without cause, and symptoms (nausea, rash, headache) are not the cause of illness. Symptoms are signals that the body is out of balance and expressions of the body's attempt to heal itself. Causes originate on many levels, but are often found in the patient's lifestyle, diet, habits, or emotional state. When only the symptoms are treated, the underlying causes remain, and the patient may develop a more serious, chronic condition.

A naturopath is a doctor who treats the whole person along the lines of the other therapies included here. The idea is to use noninvasive and nontoxic treatments. Naturopaths draw on a whole range of therapies that includes nutrition, homeopathy, acupuncture, chiropractic adjustments, and suggestions for a healthy lifestyle. Naturopathic medicine does not have thousands of names for different diseases. There are only about seven basic causes for interference with the innate natural state, the primary one being toxicity. The other causes of disease are structural imbalances, genetics, circulation, trauma, and nonphysical elements such as mental, emotional, and spiritual problems.

In 1902, the first naturopathy students in the United States graduated from the Dr. Benedict Lust School in New York. Lust said, "In this science are the disciplines common to all healing arts—a thorough study of the human organism, how it is influenced by all aspects of its environment and the techniques of discovering the nature of the disease process."

By the 1920s, there were over twenty colleges in the United States where one could study naturopathy. This number decreased in the 1940s when the strong voices in conventional medicine denounced the natural healing of naturopathy in favor of prescribed drugs. Naturopathy's popularity is now rising again.

There are six main principles in naturopathy that separate it from other types of medical treatment:

1. *Vis medicatrix naturae*: The body has a natural ability to establish, maintain, and restore health. The physician's job is to assist by removing obstacles so that an orderly healing process can occur.
2. *Tolle causum*: Identify and treat the root of the illness, not the symptoms. A symptom is the body's effort to deal with some inner disturbance.
3. *Primum no nocere* ("do no harm"): Respecting the inherent ability of the organism to heal itself, the physician must be ever mindful of the consequences or side effects of treatment. The

more gentle and noninvasive the therapy, the less disruptive it will be to the patient's integral whole. Whenever possible, suppression of symptoms is avoided, as suppression may interfere with the healing process.

4. Treat the whole person, including the physical, emotional, spiritual, mental, environmental, and social factors that contribute to an individual's state of being.

5. *Docere*, doctor as teacher: The original meaning of the word "doctor" was "teacher." A physician is a facilitator for a patient's healing process. One of a physician's principal responsibilities is to educate the patient and encourage self-responsibility for health. A cooperative doctor-patient relationship has inherent therapeutic benefits.

6. Prevention is the ultimate goal of the naturopath. Health is a reflection of how we choose to live. Physicians help patients recognize their choices and how those choices affect their health. The physician assesses risk factors and hereditary susceptibility to disease and makes appropriate intervention to prevent illness.

Naturopathic medicine was popular and widely available throughout the United States well into the early part of the twentieth century. But the rise of "scientific medicine," the discovery and increasing use of "miracle drugs" such as antibiotics, and the institutionalization of a large medical system primarily based (both clinically and economically) on high-tech and pharmaceutical treatments were all associated with the temporary decline of naturopathic medicine and most other methods of natural healing by mid-century.

Naturopathy is related to holistic medicine, but the educational requirement for it is more intensive and in-depth. Over 4,400 hours are required of study, and students must then pass the Naturopathic Licensing Exam (NPLEX) before they become registered naturopathic doctors (NDs). Naturopathic physicians can perform minor surgery and stitch wounds, and they may also use X rays, ultrasound, and other forms of diagnostic testing.

Admission to naturopathic colleges is competitive, and students should have a bachelor's degree with some premed courses.

Looking to the Future

Today, licensed naturopathic physicians are experiencing noteworthy clinical successes, providing leadership in innovative natural medical research, enjoying increasing political influence, and looking forward to an unlimited future potential. Both the American public and policy makers are recognizing and contributing to the resurgence of the comprehensive system of health care practiced by NDs.

Naturopathic physicians are licensed as primary health care providers in Alaska, Arizona, Connecticut, Hawaii, Maine, Montana, New Hampshire, Oregon, Utah, Vermont, and Washington. In the District of Columbia, naturopathic physicians must register in order to practice. Legal provisions allow the practice of naturopathic medicine in several other states. In Canada, naturopathic physicians are also recognized in the provinces of Alberta, British Columbia, Manitoba, Ontario, and Saskatchewan.

In some areas where they are welcomed, NDs can earn almost as much as MDs.

Supplementary Therapies

6

This section deals with therapies that are either new and developing or have been used in conjunction with the primary systems of alternative care. They are listed as supplementary because there is no formal regulation or certification nationally or by a state agency. Some of these techniques are ancient while others have evolved from traditional therapies. It is important even when you practice a particular therapy to know as much as possible about other therapies. A well-versed practitioner draws from as many sources as possible.

The following therapies deal with ailments from head (cranial-sacral work) to toe (reflexology) and everything in between: eyes (iridology), ears (ear coning), nose (aromatherapy), and much more. Most forms of healing listed in this section are not separately licensed. Health care professionals must practice such therapies under their licensed title of massage therapist, acupuncturist, or chiropractor. All of these supplementary therapies can be developed into full-time successful careers.

Aromatherapy

Smell is one of the five human senses. Olfactory nerves go directly to the brain. Certain odors will connect you to experiences you may have long forgotten by stimulating the nerve centers directly without mental interpretation. Researchers claim that there are probably more types of smells than there are colors, sounds, tastes, and textures.

Aromatherapy is the science of using smells to heal. It uses the essential oils of botanicals as its basis. The essential oil is the essence of the plant, flower, or bark, extracted through a distillation process. Heat and pressure are applied to a chamber containing a large quantity of a particular substance. After a long period of time, the essential alcohol, esters, terpins, and other liquid chemical constituents of the plant are pressed out of it into another chamber.

Most essential oils also have antibacterial, antiviral, and antifungal properties and can be used for the treatment of various conditions. Essential oils can be inhaled, applied topically, and, in some cases, ingested in very small doses. In France, aromatherapy is recognized as a system of medicine and is used in hospitals.

Recent studies have shown that aromatherapy can be successful in alopecia areata (patchy, inflammatory hair loss). Eighty-six patients were randomly divided into two groups: The aromatherapy group massaged essential oils (thyme, rosemary, lavender and cedarwood) in a mixture of carrier oils daily into their scalp while the control group used only carrier oils for their daily massage. Forty-four percent of the patients in the aromatherapy group showed improvement compared to 15 percent of the patients in the control group. Other studies published recently show that essential oils used in childbirth increase contractions and alleviate anxiety, pain relief, mood, nausea, and vomiting.

Bach Flower Therapy

Bach flower therapy is a sort of combination of aromatherapy and homeopathy. Early in the 1900s, a British physician, Edward Bach, discovered that the essences of certain native flowers contain a profound power to influence the emotional states that contribute to health and illness. He developed a total of thirty-eight flower essence remedies to affect emotional states. These remedies are preserved in alcohol, and very little is needed to have a profound effect. Practitioners are trained to analyze personality types and then give the appropriate remedy. Being trained as a Bach flower therapist is an intensive process of self-discovery. Bach inspired other people to develop similar products. Major companies have been formed as a result of investigations into a whole range of products, including mineral and light essences.

Bach's flower remedies are listed in the *Homeopathic Pharmacopeia* by the U.S. Food and Drug Administration.

For more information on Bach flower therapy, contact:

Nelson Bach USA, Ltd.
Education Department
Wilmington Technology Park

100 Research Drive
Wilmington, MA 01887
(800) 319-9151
(978) 988-3833
Web site: http:// www.nelsonbach.com

Bioenergetics

This therapy was originally based on Wilhelm Reich's belief that the body is made of subtle energies and that emotions are held in specific places in the body. Reich, a student of Sigmund Freud, came to the United States and developed his own body-oriented psychotherapy.

Picking up on Reich's work, two doctors, Alexander Lowen and John Pierrakos, set up the Institute of Bioenergetics in 1956. It focuses on the physical aspects of the body in order to enhance mental health.

For more information, contact:

International Institute for Bioenergetic Analysis
155 Main Street, Suite 304
Brewster, NY 10509
(845) 279-8474
Web site: http://www.bioenergetic-therapy.com

Philadelphia Institute for Bioenergetic
    Analysis, Inc.
100 West Evergreen Avenue
Philadelphia, PA 19118
(215) 242-3232

Core Energetics

John Pierrakos broke away from Lowen in the 1970s and with his wife, Eva, formed the more spiritually based therapy of Core Energetics. It combines Reichian body-work psychotherapy with spiritual perception in trance sessions, called the Pathwork. It recognizes the body's subtle energy system as a tool for diagnosis and healing.

The technique is based on three main principles: The person is a whole physical-emotional-spiritual unit; the source of healing lies within the self; and all existence forms a unit that is evolving toward its creative destiny.

Requirements: Students interested in studying Core Energetics must be involved in some therapeutic practice—such as bodywork, chiropractic, or osteopathy—before entering the program.

Curriculum: Infrequent meetings that can take up to four years to complete.

For more information on Core Energetics, contact:

Institute of Core Energetics East
115 East 23rd Street, 12th Floor
New York, NY 10010
(212) 982-9637

Institute of Core Energetics West
Life Rhythm
P.O. Box 806
Mendocino, CA 95460
(707) 937-1825
e-mail: life@liferhythm.com
Web site: http://www.liferhythm.com

Breathing as Therapy

Breath is the source of all life. We get most of our vital energy from the air we breathe. Cessation of breathing is cessation of life itself.

All healing traditions involve the breath in some way. Most people do not breathe to the depth and capacity of which they are capable. The following therapies focus on the breath as a way of bringing more energy to the body.

B.R.E.T.H. (Breath Release Energy for Transformation and Healing)

This process was founded by an Australian woman, Kamala Hope Campbell. She believes that past traumatic experiences remain in the body and the unconscious and are at the root of many fearful and defensive decisions that create conflict in our lives. This technique of breathing and grounding of energy allows healing of past trauma to occur through love and acceptance.

B.R.E.T.H. training is offered around the United States. For more information, call (505) 466-0426.

Holotropic Breathe Work

This is a powerful method of self-exploration and healing developed by Stanislav Grof and Christina Grof, using breathing as a means of altering states of consciousness. The technique comes out of the Grofs' work with mind-altering substances. They believe that altered states lead to personal transformation. The word holotropic is taken from the Greek *holos* which means "whole" and *trepin* for "movement." It literally implies a movement toward wholeness. This work facilitates access to many levels of the human psyche, including unfinished postnatal sequences, psychological death and rebirth, and an entire spectrum of transpersonal experiences.

For more information on holotropic breathe work, contact:

Grof Transpersonal Training
PMB 516
38 Miller Avenue
Mill Valley, CA 94941
(415) 383-8779
e-mail: gtt@dnai.com
Web site: http://www.holotropic.com

Rebirthing

Rebirthing, begun by Leonard Orr, inspired the focus on conscious connective breathing. Orr has reached tens of thousands of people with this technique to release birth trauma and other unresolved emotional issues.

During a session, a therapist guides a client through a specific breathing pattern. The client may start to feel lightheaded or confused or may just start to feel some long-held emotions. As this happens, the practitioner is there to reassure and assist the person to work through his or her problems and release them from the body.

Training: To be qualified, you have to master the process.

Certification: Available only through certain training centers.

For more information on rebirthing, contact:

Rebirth International
Philadelphia Rebirthing Center
1027 69th Avenue
Philadelphia, PA 19126
(215) 424-4444
e-mail: rebirther@aol.com

Continuum

This is a creative movement modality that began in 1967 by Emilie Conrad out of her love for primitive dance. She says: " We do not move, we are movement. What we call body is not matter, it's movement. The fluids in our cells are the liquid presence of our spiritual birthright."

The basic premise of this therapy is that movement is something we are, not something we do. Continuum teaches a person to enliven himself or herself from the inside. As this happens, the person's dynamic expression in the world increases. It urges life to flow through new creative channels. This is done by encompassing the subtlety of breath, the movement of soft tissue, rapport with a partner, and undulating movement of the spine. Conrad believes that the more dynamic our movements are, the more creative we become. This is because the variety of movement we express opens up a greater variety of innate intelligence in us. One of the main focuses of Continuum is that it is not a method of moving but an ongoing evolving process of self-discovery. Conrad says: "What I see as body is the urging of creative flux, waves of fertility. This therapy has been known to help those who are severely injured and who have been immobile for years." This work can increase your own awareness of your own needs and those of your clients.

For more information, contact:

Continuum
1629 18th Street, Number 7
Santa Monica, CA 90404
(310) 453-4402
Web site: http://www.continuummovement.com

Cranial-Sacral Therapy

The movement of cerebral spinal fluid (CSF) was discovered by Dr. William Sutherland, when he was a student of osteopathy under Dr. Andrew Taylor Still. Sutherland, using himself as a guinea pig, found that the way the CSF moves through the brain is controlled by the cranium (the individual bones of the head) and its rhythmic connection to the base of the spine, the sacrum. He realized a disruption to the CSF along the spinal column, caused by trauma, underlies many internal and mental ailments. He claimed that "diaphragmatic respiratory movement is secondary to the cranial respiratory movement." He felt that this movement was an essential feature of human life and health.

This valuable therapy probably would have been lost if it weren't for John Upledger in the mid-1970s. Upledger took this technique out of the hands of fading old-time osteopaths loyal to Sutherland and created a widely popular healing technology.

Cranial-sacral therapy involves a gentle manipulation of the bones of the skull and sacrum that allows the internal rhythms to come into harmony. This gives the body the ability to make its own "self correction" to treat a wide range of conditions that include headaches, ear infections, strokes, spinal cord injuries, and cerebral palsy. This is a good complementary technique for bodyworkers, chiropractors, and even nurses.

There are internal movements of these bones that have a subtle pulsation of their own. What causes disruption to this movement is "trauma." There are several types of trauma. The first is birth trauma. The first breath of life must be full or else it can lead to problems later in life. Emotional trauma also can show physical effects. This therapy helps clear these old restrictions in the body that are housed in the spinal cord.

For more information on cranial-sacral therapy, contact:

Cranial Academy
8202 Clearvista Parkway, Suite #9D
Indianapolis, IN 46256
(317) 594-0411
Web site: http://www.cranialacademy.com

The Upledger Institute
11211 Prosperity Farms Road, Suite D-325
Palm Beach Gardens, FL 33410-3487
(561) 622-4334
e-mail: upledger@upledger.com
Web site: http://www.upledger.com

Ear Coning

This is an ancient process of clearing and cleansing the ear passages. Throughout the world, cultures have utilized various forms of ear cones to facilitate deep levels of healing, cleansing, and transformation.

Process: A hollow cloth candle is lit and placed in the opening of the ear creating a long passage way from the interior of the ear to the top of the cone. A vacuum is created that gently sucks debris, excess wax fungus, and bacteria from the ear canal and sinuses. This is known as the chimney effect.

Cones are made from 100 percent unbleached cotton, beeswax, and selected essential oils and extracts.

Benefits of Ear Coning

- Great emotional calming effect
- The ability to alleviate allergies, hearing loss, earaches, and tinnitus
- Opens and aligns vital energy flow
- Assists the cleaning of the lymphatic system and sinuses
- Enhances your senses of hearing, vision, taste, and smell

- Enhances color and spatial perception
- Removes accumulated materials that can often obstruct the ear's nerve endings restoring direct enervation to the ear and all of the corresponding reflex areas to the entire body

The process for both ears usually takes approximately one hour total. Most people find this experience deeply relaxing. This is a great adjunct to any other therapy and can be a full-time occupation as well.

For more information, contact:

Coning Works
2370 West Highway 89A, Suite 11-144
Sedona, AZ 86336
(520) 282-7812

Energy Healing

Energy healing is one of the oldest and most common forms of healing we have. It is most essential to who we really are. Everything is energy, even though that is hard to define. But bang your leg and you instantly move to hold it—you are giving yourself an energy healing.

David Bohm, the great physicist of the twentieth century, talked about how matter is just a ripple in the great sea of energy. "A healer is someone who heals by the manipulation of energy," says Jeffrey Yuen, a Taoist teacher from the Swedish Institute of Massage.

Many forms of energy healing have been handed down from generation to generation. Chinese healers have been doing this type of healing for thousands of years. Qigong is a form of exercise that builds up the healing energies. Reiki and polarity are recent forms of what some call the "laying-on-of-hands." Other forms can be seen in the cave paintings of southern France and in Egyptian temples.

The idea behind this is that illness occurs when your aura or energy body has holes, tears, or rips. When this happens, your energy is drained, leaving you vulnerable. The intention of a healer is to tap into the universal energies that bring a greater life force to the human body.

Barbara Brennan, who runs a very successful energy healing school on Long Island, says that the most important thing a person has to do in order to be a healer is to first clear away his or her own issues. The key in clearing out your own issues is that you discover the very nature of healing and can bring that energy in to help others heal. Brennan says: "If the healer hasn't been there the healer can't take you there."

There are many schools throughout the country that have programs ranging from a weekend workshop to four years in many forms of old and new techniques.

Training: A four-year program meets five times for five days in a year.

Earnings: Upon graduation you are a certified healer and can earn from $75 to $150 per session.
For more information, contact:

The Barbara Brennan School of Healing
500 N.E. Spanish River Boulevard, Suite 108
Boca Raton, FL 33431-4559
(800) 924-2564
Web site: http://www.barbarabrennan.com

The Barbara Brennan School of Healing is one of the most extensive and comprehensive programs in the country dealing with energy healing. The courses focus on psychodynamics, body-centered emotions, Core Energetics, spiritual training, meditation, anatomy, and physiology. Most important, there is great attention paid to an in-depth look at your own life and the reasons behind your feelings and motivations.

Feng Shui

Feng Shui (pronounced "fung shway") is a 4,000-year-old Eastern art of creating harmony in interior and exterior design. This ancient Chinese art of placement is the hottest new system of healing for both the internal and external parts of ourselves. The study of Feng Shui includes a broad range of subjects and is considered one part of the eight branches of Chinese medicine: acupuncture, herbal medicine, exercise (external as in martial arts and internal as in Qigong), diet, moxibustion, meditation, astrology, and Feng Shui.

Feng Shui means "wind and water": The two forces that shape the land around us. The ancient Chinese sages studied the land to locate the most beneficial flow of energy, or chi. They applied the principles of acupuncture to the physical environment. Both practices seek to establish the most harmonious flow of energy. The right placement creates the most beneficial chi, because the environment that we live in affects the way we are.

The basic premise of Feng Shui is that structures—rooms, houses, landscape—can be divided into eight parts called the Ba Qua. Each part is related to a different area of your life: career, knowledge, health, wealth, fame, marriage, children, and friends. By making a special arrangement of things you can profoundly affect that aspect of your life.

The three major concepts of Feng Shui are the flow of energy; the balance of yin and yang; and the interaction of the five elements in the universe: fire, earth, metal, water, and wood. The flow of energy is expressed in nature, where perfectly straight lines occur only in very short segments, such as sugar cane and bamboo stalks. Even the tallest trees have irregularities, and it is a natural law that energy flows in wavy lines similar to breezes and streams. When energy travels in a straight path, as in the case of a roaring flood, its awesome power is unleashed. When a flood destroys everything in its path, it usually follows something man-made, such as a road. Freeways, tunnels, bridges, buildings, and lamp-posts have straight edges that are conduits of negative energy called *sha* or "killing" energy. In Feng Shui, straight lines and the angles they create are called "killing" arrows.

The second important concept is the duality of the universe, expressed in the yin-yang symbol of one dark and one light teardrop positioned in a circle. A fluid S-shaped line divides the two teardrops and personifies the balance within the universe, nature, the environment, and the self. It is our task to maintain the balance of yin and yang within our physical, mental, emotional, spiritual, and intellectual selves. A greater understanding of this concept can be found under the Chinese medicine description in the previous chapter.

The third concept includes the five universal elements, each of which relates to the others in two ways: a generative or creative connection that provides strength and power, and an overpowering or destructive relationship that denies strength and power. Knowledge of these relationships is critical in Feng Shui; placement based on misinformation or ignorance can result in an effect opposite to the one you want to achieve.

Healers in the old school of Chinese medicine needed to know the proper Feng Shui in order to give their patients the most beneficial treatments. Even today in China, construction of the most important office buildings are not even begun until a Feng Shui expert is consulted.

It is reported that in Hong Kong no one will work for a company if the building is not built or adjusted according to Feng Shui. Even U.S. companies like Chase Manhattan Bank and Citibank, with branches in Hong Kong, Singapore, and Taiwan, have had to build their offices according to these principles before local employees would agree to work in the buildings.

Various schools of Feng Shui exist. One school works with a compass, using precise measurements and calculations. A second school relies on some basic guidelines and then infuses intuition into the decision-making process. Other schools have more modern integrative interpretations, for example, using streets to represent modern-day rivers. Still others focus on either external Feng Shui as in landscaping or internal as in interior decorating. The interior aspect of Feng Shui which is based on the "black hat school" (combining traditional Feng Shui principles) is very popular in major U.S. cities.

Becoming an expert in Feng Shui requires a life-long study, but just a little study can have great effects. Feng Shui consultants are in high demand and ask high prices for their work. Courses vary in length from months to years.

Food Therapies

Where good health is concerned, the importance of a proper diet has been largely ignored in modern society. Among our ancestors, particular foods were made for healing. For instance, early Mediterranean cultures knew garlic was a natural antibiotic. Hippocrates said: "Let food be your medicine and let your medicine be your food." Food is the source of our being.

Live Food (Raw Food Diet)

The latest craze of healing food diets is the live food diet. This the belief that uncooked, fresh, and even sprouted foods are the best for you. There are many Web sites that provide information on live foods, and educators such as David Wolfe give classes around the country about this vibrant, healthy approach to eating.

David Wolfe's Raw Foods
(800) 205-2350
e-mail: nature@rawfood.com
Web site: http://www.rawfood.com/eden7.html

An older and more conservative approach to the raw diet was given by Ann Wigmore. She was one of the first in the West to find that eating live foods provided the most essential and active enzymes for life. She insists on cutting out all foods that are not living. That means avoiding all processed foods, breads, meats, and even cooked grains and vegetables. Her diet is composed primarily of raw fruits and vegetables, sprouted grains, and plenty of green vegetable juices. A major daily requirement is wheatgrass juice. It is made from the juice of sprouted wheat berries and is full of chlorophyll. By following this diet for weeks at a time, people at her institute "detox" and start to heal from many chronic diseases.

For more information on food therapy, contact one of the following:

Ann Wigmore Institute
P.O. Box 429
Rincón, Puerto Rico 00677
(787) 868-6307
Web site: http://www.annwigmore.org

Hippocrates Health Institute
1443 Palmdale Court
West Palm Beach, FL 33411
(561) 471-8876
Web site: http://www.hippocratesinst.com

The Option Institute and Fellowship
2080 South Undermountain Road
Sheffield, MA 01257-9643
(413) 229-2100
e-mail: info@optioninstitute.com
Web site: http://www.option.org

Macrobiotics

Macrobiotics, a term used in ancient Greece, refers to the art of maintaining health and longevity through living in harmony with the environment. In modern times, the term was recovered by Japanese philosopher George Ohsawa. He used it to represent a healthy way of life. Macro means "large" or "great," and bios means "life." To be macrobiotic is to experience "the great life." Michio and Aveline Kushi, students of George Ohsawa, brought macrobiotics to North America from Japan in the 1960s. They were in large part responsible for sparking the health food industry in the United States.

The principles of macrobiotic eating are based on the Oriental philosophies of yin, yang, and being. A macrobiotic eats only what is locally grown in order to keep in touch with the environment. The macrobiotic diet is a high-fiber, low-protein, complex-carbohydrate diet. Although the specific diet is tailored for each individual, it basically consists of 50 percent grains, 25 percent cooked vegetables, 10 percent beans, 10 percent sea vegetables, 5 percent soup, and occasionally some fish.

For more information on macrobiotics, contact:

The Kushi Institute
P.O. Box 7
Becket, MA 01223
(800) 975-8744
e-mail: programs@kushiinstitute.org
Web site: http://www.macrobiotics.org

Iridology

Not only are the eyes the windows to the soul, they are the windows into the health of the body as well. In iridology, the irises of the eyes are seen as a map through which an observer can determine the health or weakness of the various systems of the body. Many health care professionals use iridology as an additional tool for diagnosis.

By using a bright light and a magnifying lens, an iridologist gauges the fiber quality of the iris, which represents the body's constitutional strength. There are specific wreaths around each pupil that correspond to the autonomic nervous system, the stomach, and nutrient absorption. The presence of a milky white rim around the outer edge of the iris can indicate high sodium or cholesterol levels. Other lines and lesions can suggest inherited weaknesses, lymphatic congestion, or problems with the elimination of toxins.

Dr. Bernard Jensen, a founding father of many alternative therapy practices including colonic therapy, created charts indicating where the body is reflected in the iris. Jensen says that not only are the conditions of major organs revealed in the eye, but inflammations, bowel conditions, allergies, and areas of the brain that deal with motor and sense activity are also reflected.

Certification programs in iridology are reviewed and approved by national and international associations. Most are designed for health care professionals.

Polarity Therapy

Polarity was founded by an Austrian doctor, Dr. Randolph Stone, who was born in 1890. Stone studied chiropractic, osteopathy, and naturopathy. Stone had a unique interest in healing systems from all over the world. He observed many cultures and paid particular attention to three Eastern modes: the Chinese acupuncture system, the Indian Ayurvedic system, and the ancient Egyptian or Hermetic Wisdom Teachings. Polarity as we know it today was Stone's synthesis of his knowledge and experience of Eastern and Western healing systems.

Polarity teaches that humans are fields of pulsating energy made up of specific frequencies of life energy known as the five elements. These elements are ether, air, fire, water, and earth. Each element relates and flows in a balance of positive, negative, and neutral attractions. When our thoughts and emotions are out of alignment with the energy requirements of a life event, an imbalance of life energy results. Energy imbalances may lead to confusion, pain, emotional discomfort, and other physical symptoms. Over a long period of time, energy imbalances may appear as clinical disease. Polarity teaches that the pain and discomforts of life are signals for us to learn and that they present an opportunity to change and realign our lives.

In polarity therapy, the practitioner places his or her left hand on the tender spot and the right hand on the opposite side of the body. This procedure balances the whole body. A treatment session usually lasts an hour or more.

The American Polarity Therapy Association (APTA) accredits schools and training programs. A student must complete 155 hours of an accredited program and 615 hours of training certification by a registered polarity practitioner (RPP).

For more information, contact:

American Polarity Therapy Association
P.O. Box 19858
Boulder, CO 80308
(303) 545-2080
Web site: http://www.polaritytherapy.org

Reflexology

Reflexology is based on the idea that the bottom of the foot is a microcosm of the body. Laura Norman, who has done a tremendous job in bringing greater public awareness to reflexology and its health benefits, declares that it "can produce a state of relaxation deeper than other forms of bodywork." Stimulating certain areas of the sole of the foot will have a reflex reaction on the corresponding organs of the body. This is shown on Egyptian scrolls over 5,000 years old.

Reflexology can be used as a complementary therapy, but many people make it their specific calling, because working on the foot can speed up healing in any part of the body. For instance, to relieve problems in the reproductive systems of men or women, you would work on the ankle and the inner and outer heel because corresponding positions on the foot mirror corresponding positions in the body. Most people don't realize that there are 1,400 mechanisms working in the feet. Each foot has 26 bones, 107 ligaments, 19 muscles, and over 7,000 nerve endings. This type of drugless therapy creates a physiological change in the body by naturally improving your circulation, which reduces your body tension and enhances relaxation. It aids in the elimination of body waste and restoring the body functions to better health.

Reflexology is also used for preventative health care by relieving the body of stress. It can also be used for alleviating pain, cleansing the body, curing addictions, and improving circulation.

There are weekend courses that are good introductions or year-long certification programs. Treatment sessions range from $50 to $80, depending on the city in which they are offered.

For more information on reflexology, contact:

Reflexology Association of America
4012 Rainbow, Suite K-PMB#585
Las Vegas, NV 89103-2059
(702) 871-9522
Web site: http://www.reflexology-usa.org

Reiki

Reiki is derived from the Japanese words *ray* for "divine wisdom" and *ki* for "life-force energy." It is said to be an ancient Tibetan healing method that was rediscovered by Japanese spiritual seeker Dr. Mikao Usui in the nineteenth century. Reiki has recently become popular as a hands-on healing method of projecting energy. Practitioners become channels for allowing a particular aspect of healing energies to flow through them.

A study published in the *Journal of Subtle Energies & Energy Medicine* in 1998 showed that Reiki is an effective modality for reducing pain, depression, and anxiety. Reiki is effective in enhancing positive personality changes such as decreased trait anxiety, increased self-esteem, and a greater sense of internal control.

There are three levels of proficiency to attain. The first level costs from $100 to $200; the second level, $200 to $300; and the third level, around $500.

Shamanic Healing

With the publication of books by Carlos Castenada and Lynn Andrews, shamanism has become a part of popular culture. But shamanism is the root of all religions world wide. It went hand-in-hand with herbology and other types of physical healing. However, shamanism focuses on the deeper spiritual aspects of a person's health. This type of therapy includes a combination of herbs, fasting, breathing exercises, drumming, singing, and prayer. Shamans attempt to restore harmony between a person and the spiritual world by inducing altered states of awareness.

In the book *The Way of the Shaman*, Michael Harner says that shamans were "keepers of a remarkable body of ancient techniques that they used to achieve and maintain well-being and healing for themselves and members of their community." Harner and students like Sandra Ingerman train people in this ancient technique of healing.

For more information on shamanic healing, contact one of the following:

The Foundation for Shamanic Studies
P.O. Box 1939
Mill Valley, CA 94942
(415) 380-8282
Web site: http://www.shamanism.org

Hawaiian Shamanic Training
P.O. Box 665
Kilauea, HI 96754
(808) 828-0302

Lynn Andrews Center for Shamanic Arts
    and Training
1396 Skillman Lane
Petaluma, CA 94952
(707) 765-0733
Web site: http://www.lynnandrews.com

Shiatsu (Acupressure or Japanese Healing Massage)

Shiatsu comes from the Japanese words *shi*, meaning "finger," and *atsu*, meaning "pressure." It combines the principles of Chinese medicine with practices similar to those of acupuncture, but is performed without needles. Instead it uses a variety of other techniques, including pressing, hooking, sweeping, shaking, rotating, grasping, vibrating, patting, plucking, lifting, pinching, rolling, and brushing.

The roots of shiatsu can be traced back to the tenth century, when Japanese monks began to study Buddhism in China. They observed the healing methods of Chinese medicine and took them back to Japan. There, they not only adopted the whole system, they enhanced its methods in new combinations, eventually achieving a unique Japanese form called shiatsu. Like the Japanese transformation of the

107

Chinese tea ceremony and flower arrangement, shiatsu became uniquely Japanese.

In the 1950s and 1960s, Shizuto Masunaga, a Japanese psychologist and student of Zen, reincorporated psychological and spiritual dimensions into shiatsu. In the early 1970s, a few Japanese practitioners, including Masunaga's protégé Wataru Ohashi, came to the United States to teach shiatsu to Americans.

Continual diagnosis is an integral part of shiatsu treatment. The healing energy and awareness build in this synergy for both practitioner and client. As Wataru Ohashi describes: "The giver is the receiver, the receiver the giver." The cost of a shiatsu session can range from $50 to $125.

Sound Healing

Ancient seers used sound as a medium to heal, support, center, empower, and expand consciousness. Sound healing uses toning, chanting, or vibrations from the voice or instruments to stimulate the body's own ability to heal itself. Certain sounds and music are known to boost the immune system, regulate respiration, lower blood pressure, alleviate pain, reduce stress, and promote endurance. Practitioners work with the belief that each cell in the body is a sound resonator and has its own pulse, pattern, and cycle.

The healing power of some natural sounds has been known for centuries. In south India, farmers believe that humming and buzzing insects guarantee healthy sprouting of the sugar cane. Carefully conducted experiments have proven that plants grow faster when music is piped over fields or into greenhouses. Germination, growth, flowering, fruiting, and seed yield are affected by sound waves, especially musical sounds in the low frequency range, from 100 Hz to 600 Hz. Farm animals and pets have been known to respond to music. For example, cows give more milk when music is relayed to the milking parlor. If plants and animals respond to music, it is quite possible humans may do the same. It would be useful to extend research in this area to find out whether this is the case.

Sound or music therapy is now used by health professionals in private practices, hospitals, schools, nurseries, birthing centers, hospices, and psychotherapeutic settings. New York's hematologist-oncologist doctor Mitchell Gaynor prescribes the healing tones of Tibetan bowls along with chemotherapy to put patients back on the road to health.

The scientific explanation is quite simple. Most bodily functions—including temperature, thirst, hunger, blood sugar levels, and growth—are regulated by the hypothalamus. The hypothalamus also regulates sleeping, walking, sexual arousal, and emotions such as anger and happiness.

When we hear a sound, an immediate message to the hypothalamus also goes to the brain's limbic system, which processes emotions, and to an area called the hippocampus, the part of the brain responsible for memory. This is the reason why certain sounds bring back past memories and have such powerful effects on us.

Some schools have music therapy degrees, and other schools have practitioner certificate training programs.

Many other healing arts programs include elements of sound in their curriculum. Master's degrees are required from those practitioners trained in music therapy or counseling education.

Thai Massage

Thai massage is gaining popularity in North America, because it is fun and can be learned in a weekend. There are six-month courses in Thailand, but overall even a short course can provide effective training.

Thai medicine is strongly influenced by both the Ayurvedic traditions of India and the various traditions of China. The physical medicine, or massage part, of the tradition is called Nuad Bo'Rarn.

This practice involves a lot of stretching, and prime importance is placed on the abdominal region. According to Thai medicine, all the major pathways of the body have their origin in the abdominal region. There is also a very deep penetrating technique that works with the client's pain endurance. For this reason, the movements are practiced very slowly, with both the practitioner and the client in a heightened or meditative state of consciousness.

Nuad Bo'Rarn is the Buddhist application of "loving kindness" (*metta*). It places emphasis on the mind-body connection and on fulfilling the Buddhist ideals of compassion, loving kindness, vicarious joy, and equanimity. This technique can be used by many massage therapists and other bodyworkers. Each session, which can take two to three hours, contains over 130 different moves.

Trager Therapy

The Trager Approach is the innovative learning system of movement re-education created and developed over the past sixty-five years by Milton Trager, M.D. Each part of the client's body is moved rhythmically so that he or she experiences the possibility of moving lightly, effortlessly, and freely on his or her own. A Trager session should help reduce stress from chronic tension, teach more effective ways to recover from stressful situations, enhance conscious awareness and flexibility, improve self-image, expand energy, and restore free-flowing movement and full self-expression by reducing constriction and rigidity.

Sessions lasts from one to one and a half hours. No oils or lotions are used and the client is dressed in swimwear or briefs. During the session the practitioner moves the client gently and in such a way that the client experiences an effortless movement of his or her own. This effortless movement is then reinforced by mentastics, Dr. Trager's term for mental gymnastics, or "mindfulness in motion." It puts aside all effort and focuses instead on the subtle pleasures of the tissue in motion, the client, and the practitioner's positive feeling experiences to expand the "vocabulary" of the body movements. This enables the body to become an instrument for full self-expression. Milton Trager says that after a good session it seems as though the soul of the person is revealed.

Certification program: The Trager Institute's professional program takes a minimum of six months to complete. It consists of a six-day beginning training course of study for $750, a five-day intermediate training course of study for $625, and a six-day anatomy and physiology training course of study for $750. There is also a sixty-hour period of fieldwork and evaluations after the beginning training.

Treatments: An average session costs about $75 for an hour and a half session. Because many benefits of the Trager Approach are cumulative, clients most often benefit from a series of sessions.

For more information, contact:

Trager International
24800 Chagrin Boulevard, Suite 205
Beachwood, OH 44122
(216) 896-9383
e-mail: admin@trager.com
Web site: http://www.trager.com

Watsu

Developed only in the last few years, this therapy is so named because it combines water and shiatsu. The sessions take place in large tubs or pools of water that are kept at body temperature. The clients are supported by the practitioner so that they can relax in a kind of prenatal atmosphere. With the use of slight pressure on the body and a swaying action, the client is allowed to enter a different state of awareness, which facilitates an overall healing of the mind, body, and spirit.

For more information, contact:

Watsu Training
Harbin Hot Springs School of Massage
P.O. Box 782
Middletown, CA 95461
(707) 987-2477

Part III
The Future

Choosing a Therapy

Having to choose from such a wide array of therapies may seem overwhelming when you are devising a course of study. Where do you start? By doing your homework! Read the choices over again and see what sparks your interest. It may be more than one modality. In any case, pursue what interests you. Call or write to the schools in which you are interested and ask each school to send you a catalog. Read the literature carefully, then follow up with phone calls or a visit to the school.

Hints for the Right School

It is up to you to see what will satisfy your needs. Here are some guidelines to follow when looking at schools:

1. Learn about the profession, the different methods of therapy, and the particular requirements to practice in your state.

2. Collect information about several programs. Visit the school and, if allowed, sit in on a few classes. Interview current and former students and get their opinions on the school.

3. Consider your career intentions—some programs focus on gentle, easy techniques while others target remedial or medical applications.

4. Examine the credentials and experience of the faculty. Sit in on a class and try to picture yourself as an actual student there. Are you comfortable? Does the teaching style suit you?

5. Receive sessions from the faculty, graduates, and/or student clinic. This will also give you an opportunity to investigate, ask questions, and voice concerns.

6. Request information about student services like postgraduate job placement offices or tutoring and continuing education classes. Find out if there are organized student study groups and if time is available for appointments with the faculty.

7. Consider tuition, fees, any other costs, the availability of financial aid, and the quality of the program. Remember to budget in additional funds for a massage table, books, and supplies. See if the school is nationally accredited; if it is, you may be able to receive low-interest, federally funded student loans. Ask about work-study programs that can cut the cost of tuition.

8. If you do go away to school, see if it is an area where you might want to continue to live. A town with a big school has many people who continue to live there after graduating, thus making the job market in a particular field very tight. (A good example is Santa Fe, New Mexico, with 50,000 residents, 2 good acupuncture schools, and more than 200 registered acupuncturists.)

9. Find out whether the educational philosophy of the program and the faculty agree with your own views about health, healing, and the purpose of the therapy.

10. Most important of all, determine which field best fits your personal desires and how, given all your talents, you can best make a meaningful contribution to the world.

If you cannot decide on a specific field and you want to be in the healing profession, a good place to start is in a massage or a holistic health program. This is like getting a liberal arts degree, which gives you a taste of many different disciplines. Remember all schools have strong and weak points. No place is perfectly suited for everyone. You just have to make sure the pros outweigh the cons.

Admissions and Tuition

When applying to a school you usually will be expected to submit a completed form and transcripts from high school and college. The best and easiest way to help pay for the schooling of your choice is to get financial aid, which is generally a low-interest government loan that you can pay back over time upon graduating. This is only granted to those attending accredited programs.

If you think you will need assistance in paying for your education, you should speak directly with a financial aid representative. Be sure to ask about work-study programs.

Accreditation Pros and Cons

Benefits of Accredited Schools

1. Accreditation assures that the institute and programs have a clearly defined and appropriate objective.
2. Accreditation also provides recognition that the content and quality of the education offered has been evaluated extensively and meets standards established by and for professionals.
3. Some feel that accreditation stimulates institutions' self-improvement. This is because national standards are set that keep the institution up to par.
4. Accreditation also provides assurance of quality education.
5. Accreditation provides eligibility for financial aid from federal and private agencies.

Benefits of Nonaccredited Schools

1. Nonaccredited schools are generally smaller in size. This can provide more individualized attention from the instructors.

2. Nonaccredited institutions are generally cheaper and therefore more affordable to the unemployed student.

3. While financial aid is not usually available at these schools, most are still geared toward the criteria set up by the state's licensing agency. Students who graduate from these schools are generally eligible for state licensing.

Even though some schools listed in this book might not be labeled as accredited, a lot of schools are constantly applying to state regulatory agencies to gain accreditation status. So if you like a particular school and you wish to go somewhere that is accredited, always check with the school as to their current standing before you make a choice.

Alternative Medicine in the Schools

Although studies in alternative medicine have traditionally been excluded from mainstream curricula, they are becoming more commonly accepted. In fact, many medical doctors are now taking courses in alternative medicine. Also, many conventional medical programs are incorporating alternative ideas and holistic training courses into their curricula. The idea is based on the concept that the person/patient is part of a larger community—in the natural and spiritual realms. For this reason, physical health is connected with mental health and spiritual well-being. Healing can be found in the community, as well as within a person's own mind.

There are several different areas of study within the field of alternative medicine. These include mental health degree programs with a spiritual component, spiritual/religious degree programs with a mental health component, mind-body studies, and creative and expressive therapy degree programs.

Apprenticeships Versus Schools

Advantages of Apprenticeship Programs

- Apprenticeships offer more personalized attention.
- You see the art and skill of a craft up close.
- You receive practical training, whereas in schools you deal with mostly theory and information before you begin to practice.
- You can ask questions more easily.
- You will gain valuable insight from working with a professional.
- You get to see how an actual practice is run.
- The cost is usually much cheaper than it is with schools.

Disadvantages to Apprenticeship Programs

- You learn your field from only one practitioner. Sometimes it is better to be exposed to many different points of view and treatment styles in order to synthesize your own unique system of treatment.

- It is hard to find a professional who will take on an apprentice. Many are too busy, do not want to teach, or can't be bothered to deal with students.
- Not all alternative health fields lend themselves to apprenticeships, but for some therapies it is the traditional way. These include herbalists, acupuncturists, naturopaths, homeopaths, nutritionists, shamans, energy workers, and aromatherapists.

You can, of course, go to school and also be an apprentice. This can delay the start of your practice for several years. But remember that in ancient cultures it took ten years of study before someone could be considered qualified to practice an aspect of healing.

Investigating Other Resources

8

The Internet has emerged as a major source of health care information related to CAM for both consumers and health care providers. Surveys show that 30 million Americans sought health information online in 2001 and that this number is increasing dramatically. There are literally thousands of Web sites that talk about alternative medicine. In most cases you just have to enter the name of the therapy you are looking for, or use a search engine such as google.com. Listed below are just a few of the more comprehensive Web sites that give an overview of this vast topic.

About Massage

About Massage (http://www.aboutmassage.com) provides a complete listing of massage schools around the country. The site also has information on just about every massage technique there is, including acupressure, Canadian deep muscle massage, connective tissue massage, cranial-sacral therapy, reflexology (foot massage), infant massage, myofascial release, myotherapy, polarity therapy, Reiki, Rolfing, shiatsu, sports massage, Swedish massage, Thai massage, trigger point, and hundreds of other techniques.

Alternative Medicine University

The Alternative Medicine University (http://www.altmeduniversity.com) profiles alternative systems of medicines such as electro homoeopathy, Bach flower, biochemic medicines, naturopathy, hydrotherapy, chromotherapy, teletherapy, gem therapy, astrotherapy, chiropractic, osteopathy, herbal medicines, hypnosis, radiesthesia, radionics, bioenergetics, homoeopuncture, indoallopathy, magnetotherapy, urine therapy, and aromatherapy.

Center for Mind-Body Medicine

Founded by James A. Gordon, M.D., this nonprofit educational site (http://www.cmbm.org) is devoted to creating a new compassionate medicine that combines ancient healing wisdom and modern medical science. It provides information on training programs, center programs, articles, and recommended books.

The Fetzer Institute

The Fetzer Institute (http://www.fetzer.org) is a nonprofit educational organization furthering mind/body/spirit health care approaches through education and research. Its Web site provides information on the organization's philosophy, programs, resources, and events.

Health Web

Health Web (http://www.healthwwweb.com) provides educational resources and networking services to patients, practitioners, and students.

Institute of Noetic Sciences (IONS)

The Institute of Noetic Sciences (http://www.ions.org) is an organization that supports mind/body health and spiritual development in order to move towards a humanistic societal transformation. Its substantive Web site includes program publications, research publications, archives of IONS articles, events, and travel programs.

NaturalHealers.com

NaturalHealers.com (http://www.naturalhealers.com) provides a resource that allows students to compare alternative medicine schools, contact them, read common questions and answers, and ask questions. Its e-mail address is info@naturalhealers.com.

The International Society for the Study of Subtle Energies and Energy Medicine (ISSSEEM)

ISSSEEM (http://www.issseem.org) was organized for the purpose of improving human health and disseminating information to the public about subtle energies and energy medicine through the advancement of education, practice, training, and research in the emerging field of subtle energies and energy medicine.

Bookstores

In a growing field like alternative medicine, new books are published every year dealing with fresh methods of treatment and deeper investigations into old methods. Libraries can be good research facilities, but the best places to get up-to-date information on alternative medicine are bookstores. While most bookstores have a health and therapy section, you might be better off checking some of the ones that specialize in alternative ideas about health and spirituality. The Bodhi Tree in Los Angeles, The Ark in Santa Fe, East West Books in New York City, or Healing Earth Resources in Chicago are just a few of the many stores where you can find all sorts of books on the healing arts. These stores will also order and ship to you any book that is in print.

Valuable Books

Besides surfing the Internet or just browsing around a bookstore here are a few very good books that will give the prospective student a firm foundation to begin the understanding of the art and science of healing.

The Aquarian Conspiracy
Marilyn Ferguson

Although published over twenty years ago, this is still one of the most important books available for laying the ground work of holistic thinking. Ferguson weaves together a rich tapestry of the arts and sciences to come up with a possible picture of a holistic future. This is a must read for anyone attempting to understand the paradigms of thought that can shape our world in a positive direction.

Ayurvedic Healing
Dr. David Frawley

Dr. Frawley is one of the great scholars of Ayurvedic medicine. Besides running a school in Santa Fe, he explains the Ayurvedic approach to all major common health problems in this comprehensive book. In it, he also recommends the appropriate diet, herbs, oils, aromas, mantras, and meditation as required. The book contains an extensive introductory section that outlines Ayurvedic health regimens for disease prevention. Anyone interested in Ayurveda will find this book useful and will want to keep it as a reference guide for healthful living.

Between Heaven and Earth: A Guide to Chinese Medicine
Harriet Beinfield and Efrem Korngold

A great introduction to the science and study of Chinese medicine, this book includes a detailed understanding of the five elements theory, which is crucial in understanding the Chinese healing systems. It is a great place for beginners to learn the intricacies of this ancient system of medicine. *Between Heaven And Earth* opens the door to a vast storehouse of knowledge that bridges the gap between mind and body, theory and practice, professional and self-care, East and West.

Cross Currents: The Perils of Electropollution, The Promise of Electromedicine
Robert O. Becker, M.D.

Dr. Becker explains the effectiveness of alternative healing methods that use parts of the body's innate electrical healing systems and warns that our bodies are being adversely affected by power lines, computers, microwaves, and satellite dishes.

Feng Shui: Harmony by Design
Nancy Santopietro

There are now many books on the market about this popular subject. But this one is a very practical guide for understanding the basics of Feng Shui. There are floor plans for setting up offices and homes. Charts on colors and properties of gemstones, crystals, and aromatherapy oils enhance readers' acquisition of knowledge about this Chinese art. *Feng Shui* can give you great tips on improving your health, wealth, and relationships.

The Future of the Body: Explorations into the Further Evolution of Human Nature
Michael Murphy

A survey of the transformative capacities of human nature, this book emphasizes the mind-body phenomena, focusing especially on individuals who apparently have extended the usual reach of human possibility—saints, mystics, psychics, artists, geniuses, among others. In it, Murphy discusses and documents placebo effects, spiritual healing, hypnosis, somatic disciplines such as the Alexander Technique and the Feldenkrais Method, yogic powers, and the charismas of saints.

Hands of Light: A Guide to Healing Through the Human Energy Field
Barbara Ann Brennan.

Brennan runs one of the most well-respected energy healing schools in the country. Trained as a physicist and psychotherapist, she has spent the last fifteen years studying the human energy field and working as a healer. This book details a study of the human energy field and how it is connected to a person's health. It also contains essential information for anyone involved in healing and conscious health care.

Heal Your Life
Louise Hay

Heal Your Life is a comprehensive guide to the mental causes behind physical illness and injury. It offers positive ways to replace negative feelings and shows how a change in attitude can result in a permanent state of health and well-being. It is a great book to have on hand when dealing with mind-body healing.

Quantum Healing: Exploring the Frontiers of Mind/Body Medicine
Deepak Chopra, M.D.

This a book that lays out a way of thinking about alternative health care. Dr. Chopra writes about how the body is capable of doing much more than we assume it can. He calls the ability to cure disease from within "quantum healing," and shows how we are all capable of miraculous healing. Dr. Chopra believes intelligence exists everywhere in our bodies, in each of our 50 trillion cells, and that, therefore, each cell knows how to heal itself.

Sounds of Healing: A Physician Reveals the Power of Sound, Voice, and Music
Mitchell L. Gaynor, M.D.

Dr. Mitchell Gaynor, director of medical oncology at the Strang-Cornell Cancer Prevention Center in New York City, tells of his discovery of the healing power of sound through one of his patients, a Tibetan monk who taught him sacred chants and played the Tibetan singing bowls for him. The experience, he says, led him to explore harmonics as a powerful healing force. He explains the techniques he uses, the philosophy behind his integrated practice, and many healing stories of his patients.

Vibrational Medicine: New Choices for Healing Ourselves
Richard Gerber, M.D.

Dr. Gerber's research and his coverage of other people's research helps explain why energy healing works and how our bodies are vibrational energy patterns. Gerber explains current theories about how various energy therapies work and offers readers new insights into the physical and spiritual perspectives of health and disease.

Why People Don't Heal and How They Can
Caroline Myss, Ph.D.

Caroline Myss, along with Deepak Chopra, is an author whose books about health and healing continually make the best-sellers' list. They have had a profound effect on the acceptance of alternative medicine. This book is an excellent way of understanding how to go beyond limited unhealthy beliefs. A key point of Myss's is that illness can be, (but is not always) a stage in spiritual growth.

Videos

In addition to all the books, there are also many excellent videos on the market that show all sorts of beautiful techniques and philosophies of the healing arts.

The Healing Power of Flowers
by BC Video

This is a great tape about a woman who conquers a life-threatening autoimmune disease when she discovers the secret of flower essences. Also on this tape are doctors, shamans, and herbalists who integrate much of the holistic philosophy mentioned throughout this book. Visit the Web site at http://www.bcvideo.com.

Healing and The Mind
Bill Moyers

Originally seen on PBS, this six-part series goes into a deep understanding of the practical aspects of healing. It investigates many alternative approaches. The best part is part one, which deals with demonstrations in China of healing chi energy.

Alternative Medicine Network

The Alternative Medicine Network has a whole line of healing videos. Its massage video gives an overview of principles and techniques. It also has remarkable stories of patients who have brought healing and balance to their lives through the use of massage. Visit the Web site at http://www.altmednetwork.net/healingvideos.

Food Stores

A great place to learn about alternative medicine is probably right in your own town or city. Health food stores and alternative medicine help support each other in many ways. These stores are collaborators in the holistic vision of the self-empowered alternative health approach. They offer support to the field by offering many alternative medicine products, organic foods, supplements, and herbal remedies.

Some stores like Whole Foods and Wild Oats have stores throughout the country and provide excellent customer service departments where many people will talk to you about alternative medicine and their experiences. Many stores have bulletin boards that announce discussions about different healing therapies. Try going to your local health food store and asking the department managers about the areas of health you are interested in.

Retreat Centers

There are many wellness centers and retreat centers all over the country at which a prospective student may spend a weekend, a week, or the whole summer investigating many forms of alternative therapies.

These centers are not substitutes for formal education in a particular field, but they provide an opportunity for you to get your feet wet with the general ideas and practices of a particular field.

Places like the Eslan Institute in Big Sur, California, and the Omega Institute in Rhinebeck, New York, have had a major influence on the holistic/consciousness movement. In fact, these places have become the breeding grounds for the development and public presentation of new therapies. Many centers are a great mix of spirituality and health awareness.

Esalen Institute

Highway 1
Big Sur, CA 93920-9616
(831) 667-3000
e-mail: info@esalen.org
Web site: http://www.esalen.org

Harbin Hot Springs

P.O. Box 782
Middletown, CA 95461
(707) 987-2477
(800) 622-2477
Web site: http://www.harbin.org

Healing Earth Resources

3111 North Ashland Avenue
Chicago, IL 60657
(773) 327-8459
Web site: http://www.healingearthresources.com

Omega Institute of Holistic Studies

150 Lake Drive
Rhinebeck, NY 12572
(800) 944-1001
e-mail: registration@eomega.org
Web site: http://www.eomega.org

Expos/Conferences

Throughout the country, there are expos where you can have a chance to hear about and experience firsthand the type of therapy that you might like to pursue. By letting a practitioner of a particular healing art work on or with you, you can tell if you that particular type of therapy matches your interest.

New Life Expo

218 West 72nd Street
New York, NY
(212) 787-1600
Web site: http://www.newlifemag.com

The Omega Institute

Web site: http://www.eomega.org/omega/
    conferences.com

Organizations

Organizations such as the International Alliance of Healthcare Educators are coalitions of health care instructors who have developed a curriculum to advance innovative therapies through high-quality continuing education programs. The alliance currently coordinates 700 workshops per year in major cities throughout the world, in support of more than twenty modalities developed by practitioners renowned in the fields of complementary health care.

The International Alliance of Healthcare Educators (IAHE)

11211 Prosperity Farms Road, Suite D325
Palm Beach Garden, FL 33410-3487
(800) 311-9204
(561) 622-4334
Web site: http://www.iahe.com

Periodicals

There are many health periodicals in circulation around the country that report on the latest trends in health and healing. These can be found in local bookstores or in many health food stores around the country. You may contact these periodicals directly. Some are listed below.

Common Ground

3091 West Broadway, Suite 201
Vancouver, BC V6K 2G9
Canada
(604) 733-2215
(800) 365-8897
Web site: http://www.commongroundmagazine.com

New York Spirit

107 Sterling Place
Brooklyn, NY 11217
(800) 634-0989
Web site: http://www.nyspirit.com

Whole Life Times

Box 1187
Malibu, CA 90265
Web site: http://www.wholelifetimes.com

Preparing for the Field

9

If the art and science of healing and helping others feels like an exciting opportunity for you, there are some things you can do to prepare for this career.

Prerequisites

Many schools listed in this book require some background in science. Courses in biology, anatomy, and physiology are required to understand the human body. It is helpful to have a well-rounded educational foundation before you go into the field of healing. Study many different subjects, because everything you know will be useful in some way when you work with people.

The best kind of therapist, in any field, is one who understands people. This is why courses in psychology and philosophy are good to study. Literature is probably one of the best ways of understanding people and their motivations.

Some fields, like chiropractic and osteopathy, require a college degree. Other therapies, like acupuncture, require only two years of college. Some schools have no requirements at all, but attending a specialized school right out of high school is not recommended.

Moe Ginsburg, an educator from New Mexico, tells students that before pursuing a career in the healing arts, they "should get life experiences." He means that you should go out into the world and see how people live and find out for yourself what the world is all about. This will help you in ways that you may not realize at the time. You also need a certain maturity to deal with people and the problems that they bring you.

Funding

College or any further study in private schools, which all alternative medicine schools are, takes lots of money. Here are some resources that may find helpful in raising tuition. Again the Internet is a great source of information.

College Connection Scholarships: This Web site publishes information on free scholarships for under-graduate, graduate, and international students. It can be accessed at http://collegescholarships.com.

Scholarship Information at Your Fingertips: This site allows you to find private sources for which you may qualify. You can submit a form online or submit letters already formatted for completion. The URL is http://arcomputer.anthill.com.

United Scholarship Advisement: This is mainly a pay service to find appropriate grants or scholarships for individuals. However, the Web site does post several free scholarships periodically. You may access it at http://www.collegefunds.net.

Funding Focus: This site sells books about scholarships and financial aid for college education, study abroad, and vocational training. The Web address is http://fundingfocus.com.

Start Training Now

People who go into the field of health care are individuals who care about others. This is not something that can be taught in a school. You can assume that because you are investigating this area for a career, you already have some of this quality.

"Notice what you notice." A good practitioner in any field will be able to look at someone and see where they are out of balance. This is something you can practice. Look at what stands out in a person. Start looking at people more consciously.

Don't go around diagnosing conditions, but begin training at a young age by watching people and their patterns of behavior. See if you can make connections between what people eat and the way they look. Look at people's complexions and see if there is a correspondence between the way they look and the way they feel. From a Chinese medical perspective, a pale white face might mean lack of energy, which could be a sign of anemia. A red face is a sign of heat in the body, and a yellow face can mean a weak digestive system. These are not absolute meanings, but they will help you start understanding what you see as you begin noticing things about people.

Another skill you can begin developing while you're in high school is listening. You can learn the most about people by listening to their complaints. Learn patience.

Clients will not feel open enough to reveal themselves if you seem rushed or impatient. Sometimes listening is the best therapy of all.

The other side of listening is communicating. A good communicator can express ideas simply and can tell if he or she is being understood. The key to communicating is making eye contact. These are skills you can begin to cultivate now if you want to be a health care practitioner.

Start With Yourself

As someone thinking about the field of health care, start with yourself as your first patient. Give yourself the advice you might give others. If you exercise and eat a healthful diet, you will be a great example to others. It is up to you to create and maintain health for yourself. If something does not feel right in your body, investigate the causes and work on it. You create health by tuning in to your body and knowing what will make it feel good in the long run. If you start this now, your knowledge will be of great service when you begin to work with others.

Here are three simple steps to promote an attitude of health:

1. Think positively, become aware of the mind's negative chatter.
2. Break addictive patterns of behavior.
3. Do exercise, yoga, Qigong, or other movement therapies to stay in touch with your body.

Becoming
Professional

10

Once you have been trained and licensed, you are ready to begin. The first thing you need to do to be a good therapist in any profession is to make people feel comfortable. People want to know they can count on you and feel taken care of.

As a therapist, it is not helpful to preach your religious, political, or philosophical beliefs to clients. People want help, usually physical help. Your job is to be there for them and help balance their inner feelings about their lives and problems. You are there to strengthen their confidence in making the best choices in their lives.

Many of the problems people have lie in their habitual behavior. So it is important to encourage people to make healthy changes in their lifestyles, and to work on themselves outside of treatment. This means a healthier diet and environment, and a program of regular exercise. Such change can be a challenge to people's thinking, attitudes, and beliefs about themselves and the way they live. If you meet resistance, talk about the advantages of trying a different way of living.

You must be able to answer all questions candidly and in terms that can be easily understood. This means that you will tell a client that you cannot answer a question if you do not have the correct information. Cultivate a wide network of associates in related fields to whom you can direct these questions. This will also help generate business as you refer clients to other practitioners and they, in turn, refer clients to you.

At the end of each session, encourage clients to reflect on what has happened to them during the session. This will help them integrate your work into their daily lives.

How to Be a Good Therapist

Good professional therapists tell their patients how long they think a course of treatment will run. Will it be two sessions, ten sessions, or more? Be fair and work with people only as long as you think you can help them. Many practitioners give their professions a bad name by insisting that patients keep coming back when their treatments are no longer effective or by claiming that they can treat something that cannot be best treated by their particular modality.

Code of Ethics

At all times, a practitioner should behave professionally and practice ethical conduct as well as sound business practices aimed at ensuring the well-being of the client. The licensing board of New York State gives a special message to its practitioners: "The practice of a profession is a public trust, earned through education, experience, examination, and commitment on the part of the practitioner to public service. The professional carries out that trust in accord with ethical standards. Practitioners should always be conscious of their special obligations to public service and ethical conduct."

Here are some standards of practice set up for all professionals.

1. Provide an environment that is safe and comfortable for the client and that meets all legal requirements for health and safety.
2. Use standard precautions to insure professional hygienic practices and maintain a level of personal hygiene appropriate for practitioners in the therapeutic setting.
3. Wear clothing that is clean, modest, and professional.
4. Obtain voluntary and informed consent from the client prior to initiating the session.
5. Conduct an accurate needs assessment, develop a plan of care with the client, and update the plan as needed.
6. Use appropriate draping to protect the client's privacy.
7. Refer to other professionals when in the best interest of the client and/or practitioner or seek other professional advice when needed.
8. Respect the traditions and practices of other professionals and foster collegial relationships. Do not attack the reputation of any colleague.
9. Display/discuss schedule of fees that are clearly understood by the client or potential client in advance of the session.

10. Maintain accurate financial records, contracts and legal obligations, appointment records, and tax reports and receipts for at least four years.
11. Acknowledge and respect the client's freedom of choice in the therapeutic session.
12. Respect the client's right to refuse the therapeutic session.
13. Protect the interests of clients who are minors or who are unable to give voluntary consent by securing permission from an appropriate third party or guardian.
14. Solicit only information that is relevant to the professional client/therapist relationship.
15. Obtain all appropriate licensing as required by state and local governments.
16. Make sure recommended return visits are based on need, not the practitioner's financial stability.
17. Maintain the right to refuse and/or terminate service to a client who is abusive or under the influence of alcohol, drugs, or any illegal substance.

Communication and positive attitudes are important. It has been estimated that three-quarters of those who consult practitioners for the first time do so on the recommendation of someone they know.

A Few Don'ts

1. Do not encourage any behavior that seems problematic. This includes negative attitudes, addictions, or anything that seems like a harmful lifestyle choice for your client.
2. Do not suggest anything to your client that might be considered morally or ethically offensive.

This is especially true of sexual advances. It is not advisable to date a client. If you are attracted to a person with whom you have been working, your professional ethics require you to discontinue treatment and only then establish a personal relationship.

3. Do not imply that your opinion is the only correct one. Be open to other possibilities. Remember that what makes alternative health care different from much of conventional medicine is the chance for a community of practitioners to work together and approach the same problem from many angles.

4. If you are uncomfortable treating a person for any reason, you will be unable to provide good treatment. Let the person know that he or she will need to see someone else.

5. Do not exploit the trust and dependency of others, including clients, employees, and co-workers.

6. Do not engage in any sexual activity with a client. In the event that the client initiates sexual behavior, clarify the purpose of the therapeutic session, and, if such conduct does not cease, terminate or refuse the session

7. Do not exploit the professional relationship for personal or other gain.

Insurance for Practitioners

Being insured to perform whatever form of health care you practice is a good policy for both you and your clients. It is best to maintain both general liability and professional liability insurance coverage. There are a few companies around, like Eastern Special Risk Insurance Agency, that provide coverage from $100,000 to $3 million. The costs of this can vary anywhere from a few hundred to thousands of dollars depending on the policy, the practice, and the state.

For more information, contact:

Eastern Special Risk Insurance Agency
P.O. Box 218
Harvard, MA 01451
(978) 456-8200
(800) 341-1110

Practical Action

To gain respect as a practitioner, it is good to be clear about your methods and practices. First, you must give a thorough explanation of your treatment plan, the method you are going to use in dealing with your client's condition. This includes what you and the client can expect from the treatment, how many visits it will take, the overall cost including any supplements you might recommend, and at what point he or she might expect to feel better.

You should also cite how many similar cases you have treated in the past. Give the success rate and any research or clinical studies to back up your treatment plan. Let the client know of any side effects he or she might experience during the course of the treatment. It is important to be honest with people about the intended results of therapy. Dr. Alan Gaby, president of the American Holistic Medical Association, says, "I would rather have a practitioner tell me that thirty percent of the people experienced side effects than one who brushes off my questions and gets defensive. "

As you continue to practice you will build confidence. You have to convey this feeling to people. If you have confidence in the treatment modality you have studied, so will others. This will make them feel secure and able to trust your therapy.

Remember, even though a client comes to you initially to see if he or she can work with you, you are also assessing the client to see if you can work with him or her. Will the client be willing to cooperate with you and follow your suggestions? If a client is unwilling to make an effort to help himself or herself or if a client has a "fix me" attitude, it may be better to tell him or her to see someone else.

Setting Up a Practice

There are plenty of business opportunities and there is plenty of money available for alternative medical practitioners. In a recent interview, Jack Miller, president of the Pacific College of Acupuncture, appeared positive about the future for each graduate. With three campuses in San Diego, Chicago, and New York, and hundreds of Pacific College's graduates entering the job market every year, Miller said, "I tell everyone their success is guaranteed if they are willing to work hard. There is no lessening of the need for our services. Don't just sit around waiting for the phone to ring." Miller encourages building a practice: "Go out and work forty hours a week every single week. When they are just starting out maybe only five hours out of that forty are actually spent treating patients. So the other thirty-five hours should be spent marketing their services."

The beginning professional should go around giving free lectures to various different groups, telling people how great their treatments are. Miller also suggests "writing letters to community groups, men's and women's groups, sports groups, and those association that have formed around various diseases, and talk about the efficacies of your treatments. It is important to do demonstrations and work on everybody that you can."

What is also so affirming about Miller's testimony is that he says, "85 percent of those that have graduated are still in the field and still practicing. They are making a living. There is a huge range in salaries, anywhere from $20,000 to $250,000 a year. It all depends on the person's individual ambition."

Business Strategy

Some people in the healing business think that they should undercharge for their services because they are there to help others. Lewis Harrison of the Academy of Natural Healing in New York says that that kind of thinking can get you into trouble. He explains, "Either you are running a business or a charity. If you want to run a charity that's great, but don't expect financial rewards. A lot of time, money, and hard work has gone into your education: You must feel you have something to offer people!"

Harrison continues: "You are engaged in commerce. Commerce is commonly known as the common exchange of goods or services. It is important to charge for your services for many reasons. First, this is your livelihood. You have to feed yourself as well as overhead and student loans. More importantly, speaking money keeps your transactions clean. This way there are no favors owed or unwritten agreements. Money is also a great substitute for psychological transference. This is when the patients project emotions on the practitioner. This happens in friendships, but it is less likely when another dynamic is set up when money is exchanged."

Licensure

You must check with each individual state board in a particular therapy to see what the specific criteria are for obtaining a license. This will differ widely from state to state in fields like acupuncture. Some states, such as California, have very strict laws for acupuncturists. Others, like Arizona, have no laws at all for practice, although legislation is pending to create state licenses there. It is your responsibility to learn the licensing requirements in your state and to be aware of how regulations in your state can affect your rights and responsibilities as a practitioner.

Insurance for Patients

Testimony indicated increasing interest in and coverage of CAM services by employer-sponsored health plans in direct response to employee requests. Also, employers are increasingly adding CAM benefits to attract and retain employees, improve health, and comply with state mandates. Various employer-sponsored health plans provide limited coverage for certain CAM services (e.g. chiropractic care) as part of a basic benefit package.

Insurers are adapting as they realize that it is less expensive to keep people healthy through preventative care than it is to treat illness. They are also discovering that when treatment is necessary, alternative costs are often lower than traditional treatment modalities.

A few years back, the city of Seattle was promoting alternative therapy by prompting Blue Cross to offer individual subscribers a supplemental insurance plan. This plan provided access to a network of state-licensed naturopaths, acupuncturists, and homeopaths. When traditional allopathic medicine fails, Lovelace Health Systems, a traditional IIMO in New Mexico, offers referrals to alternative medicine providers of all sorts, such as Mexican folk healers.

In New York, legislators, in response to aggressive campaigns by chiropractic lobbies, signed a bill that would require health insurance companies to pay for unlimited chiropractic services. Now, in all but ten states, health insurance companies are required to pay for some chiropractic care.

Christopher Lieby, executive secretary of the New York Chiropractic Council, calls the need for insurance companies to cover alternative medicine "a freedom of choice . . . patients have a right to choose a competent professional to provide their health care and not have that dictated to them by the prejudices of individual insurance companies."

There are some companies that specifically cater to alternative-minded individuals, such as Alternative Health Insurance Services, who can be reached at (800) 966-8467, and American Western Life Insurance Company, (415) 573-8041. American Western Life Insurance offers a very generous wellness plan, with a twenty-four-hour holistic hotline and an extensive handbook filled with natural treatments.

The Future of Health Care

11

The great world leader Mahatma Gandhi said, "Be the change you want to see in the world." Your health is in your own hands. Acceptance of your individual responsibility toward health is very important for the future of any holistic health care system. But first, you need to be educated. Your education will be part of the re-education that will influence the awareness of the public.

Woodson Merell, assistant medical professor at Columbia University Medical School, said: "If you don't help patients to harness their own healing capacities, you are putting them at a significant disadvantage."

John Knowles, former president of the Rockefeller Foundation, said: "The major advance in the health of the American people will be determined by what the individual is willing to do for himself." The best medical treatments today necessitate awareness, on the part of health care practitioners as well as patients, of all treatment options possible for a given condition.

Prevention

Thomas Edison said:"The doctor of the future will give no medicine, but will interest his patients in the care of the frame, in diet, and in the cause of prevention of disease." The modern world has developed challenges to maintaining health. The air we breathe, the water we drink, many foods we eat, and the materials with which we build, furnish, and clean our homes have been proven to be harmful to our bodies. We are exposed to radiation from everyday sources such as power lines, microwaves, computer monitors, and cell phones. This is why a new holistic approach to health care will consist of people actively participating and taking care of their own health care needs, whether individually or with the help of an appropriate thera-pist. This is not a kind of health care that can be "pro-vided for" or "delivered." It has to be practiced by people on an educated and conscious level. As a health care provider, you can educate the public as to what its health care needs may be.

According to a report from the surgeon general's office, "dietary imbalances" are the leading pre-ventable contributors to premature death in the United States. The report recommends the expansion of nutrition and lifestyle modification education for all health care professionals.

Preventative care is the foundation of alternative medicine practices. Its successful practice requires that the health of an individual be acknowledged as a primary concern, which is determined above all by behavior, food, intake of toxins, and the surrounding environment.

As free and independent beings, we all have the power within us to keep ourselves healthy. The role of the therapist and health care professional is merely to assist that process. Many people are attempting to integrate their physical, mental, and spiritual well-being. If you choose to be an alternative medical practitioner, you will be a critical part of that process.

A Time of Change

The time for the complete acceptance of alternative holistic therapies is now. Many institutions are already on the way. Hospitals all over the country are providing new and improved integration of alternative therapies as a complementary service.

Holistic health clinics are being created around the country with medical doctors, acupuncturists, massage therapists, and chiropractors working side by side. "Every place doors are opening," says Dr. Betsy MacGregor, chairwoman of alternative medicine at Beth Israel Medical Center. MacGregor says that it seems as if there has been an explosion of hospital programs that combine alternative and conventional medicine in New York City. However, in many of these larger institutions, the term "alternative" is sometimes replaced by the phrase "complementary" or "integrative" medicine, describing the integration of healing therapies within a holistic care framework.

In New York, Beth Israel Medical Center and Memorial Sloan-Kettering Cancer Center have announced plans for integrative or complementary programs. Columbia-Presbyterian Medical Complementary

Care Center, an early leader in the use of holistic therapies, has a whole department of complementary care with treatment rooms for massage, visualization, therapeutic touch, and other techniques. Dr. Mehmet Oz, who pioneered the program at the hospital by using hands-on energy therapy in his surgeries, says, "Even at the most superficial level, complementary medicine can empower the patient."

A *New York Times* article on the acceptance of alternative medicine, stated: "Although some doctors on staff are skeptical about lending both resources and credibility to complementary services, an increasing number seem to be asking a different question altogether: What took so long?"

Securing the Future

It is only a matter of time before most doctors adopt an "if you can't beat them, join them" attitude. *Time* magazine ran a cover story on the rising public interest in alternative medicine. It predicted that the health care center of the twenty-first century would be staffed by conventional and alternative practitioners working alongside each other instead of being on opposite sides of the fence.

The new National Center for Complementary and Alternative Medicine will aid students who are applying for jobs in this field. The existence of this center indicates that students will find that opportunities in this field are growing. The mission of the center is "to ensure high-quality, rigorous, scientific review of complementary and alternative diagnostic and prevention

Careers in Alternative Medicine

modalities, disciplines and systems." The center's responsibility is "to study the integration of alternative treatment, diagnostic and prevention systems, modalities, and disciplines with the practice of conventional medicine as a complement to such medicine and into health care systems in the United States."

Most essentially, you must be a good role model for your clients. Practice what you preach. People will tend to trust someone who looks healthy and is filled with vitality over someone who is a bad listener or who eats a poor diet. Work continually to maintain the best quality of your own body, mind, and spirit.

Glossary

acute Having a sudden onset and lasting a short time.

antibiotics Various substances that help to inhibit or kill infections in the body. It has recently been discovered that overuse of antibiotics can adversely affect the immune system.

apprenticeship One-on-one study with a skilled teacher.

Ayurveda or Ayurvedic medicine Ancient system of medicine, developed in India, that places equal emphasis on the body and the consciousness of the individual and strives to restore internal and external harmony.

bodywork Any type of hands-on therapy.

Chinese medicine An array of different approaches to healing developed in China, including acupuncture, herbology, and massage.

chronic   Of long duration or frequent recurrence.

complementary medicine   Alternative medicine.

constituent   An element of something.

constitutional   Pertaining to the inherited genetics of the body.

conventional medicine   The healing practice of established medical professions.

deficient   Having less than needed.

detox   A way that the body discharges toxins; short for *detoxification*.

diagnosis   An evaluation of a condition in terms of an illness or disease.

Eastern medicine   The systems of medicines developed in Asian countries, such as India and China. These systems are usually holistic in nature.

energy   What all things need to move or change.

evolution   The belief that simpler things move toward more complex forms.

fluctuation   The movement of energy in an ebb and flow manner.

folk medicine   A healing practice, not organized in systems, that is usually handed down orally from generation to generation.

hara   Japanese word for the point below the navel where a person's center of energy is located.

herbology   The study of the use of herbs for medicinal purposes.

holistic medicine   A healing practice that includes the whole body in the diagnosis, treatment, and care of any type of condition.

immune system   The structures in the body that protect us from disease. Deficiencies in a person's immune system can contribute to health problems.

innate Existing in an organism from birth; native, inborn.

integrative Combines both alternative and orthodox medical practices.

life force The energy that enables all things to live.

manifestation The creation of any form.

manipulations Certain ways of moving the body for release and healing purposes.

mechanistic view The idea that the body and the universe function like machines.

microcosm The idea that the small is a miniature version of the large. For example, the cell is a microcosm of the body, and the body is a microcosm of Earth.

modality A specific therapy.

olfactory Nerves in the nose that let us smell.

paradigm A system of thought.

perspective The scope of awareness.

placebo A nonactive substance that is taken to produce an effect, usually on a psychological level.

poultice A soft, usually medicated mass of herbs that is placed externally on the body. It usually has the ability to draw out toxins from the body.

practitioner One who is practiced in the use of a particular therapy.

prana The ancient Sanskrit word for life force.

purgatives Herbs that produce evacuations of the system.

qi The Chinese word for life energy; also referred to as *chi* or *ki*.

quantum physics Study of physics that deals with the smallest parts of the universe.

remedy Any substance or procedure taken to cure an illness.

root cause Something that is an origin or source.

salve Like a poultice, it is made from herbs for external application but is usually mixed with beeswax or vegetable oil to preserve the mixture.

sedate To control a condition by releasing the invasion of external pathogens.

shaman One who uses altered states of consciousness to induce healing.

shen Chinese word for vitality or spirit.

spiritual What is not of the body; the intelligence of the life force.

subcutaneous Used or made under the skin.

symptom Signal from the body that there is a problem.

synergy Combined effects of things that are greater than a single effect.

Tao The way or the harmony of the universe.

tonifying To control a condition by building up deficient energies in the body.

toning The vocalization of tones or sounds without forming words.

toxins Poisons.

traditional Chinese medicine (TCM) World's oldest continuously practiced system of medicine, comprised of various therapies, that was codified in the mid-1900s by Mao Tse Tung and the Chinese Communist Party.

vibration The movement or pulsing of energy.

vitality The amount of life force in an organism.

the West Mainly the countries of America and western Europe.

Western medicine The tradition of medicine that began with Hippocrates in ancient Greece and is currently the main practice in Western countries.

yang   The male aspect of energy, also meaning light, hard, and angular.

Yellow Emperor   Legendary founder of the Chinese civilization.

yin   The female aspect of energy, also meaning dark, soft, and round.

For More Information

While many schools provide a variety of alternative therapy education, there is usually one primary teaching at a particular school.

All schools have their strong and weak points. No place is perfectly suited to everyone. You just have to be certain that the pros outweigh the cons. This is the job of the prospective student. Before registering for any course, you should research, investigate, and make sure that an institution will provide the education that you desire.

Acupuncture Schools and Colleges

ARIZONA

Arizona School of Acupuncture and Oriental Medicine
Masters of Acupuncture
Masters of Acupuncture and Oriental Medicine
4646 East Fort Lowell Road, Suite 105
Tucson, AZ 85712
(520) 795-0787
Web site: http://www.azschacu.edu

Phoenix Institute of Herbal Medicine and Acupuncture
Master of Science in Oriental Medicine
Master of Science in Acupuncture
P.O. Box 2659
Scottsdale, AZ 85252-2659
(480) 994-3648
Web site: http://www.pihma.com

Rainstar University
4120 North Goldwater Boulevard, Suite 110
Scottsdale, AZ 85251
(480) 423-0375
Web site: http://www.rainstargroup.com

CALIFORNIA

Academy of Chinese Culture and Health Sciences
Master of Science in Traditional Chinese Medicine
1601 Clay Street
Oakland, CA 94612
(510) 763-7787
e-mail: acchs@best.com
Web site: http://www.acchs.edu

American College of Traditional Chinese Medicine
Master of Science in Traditional Chinese Medicine
455 Arkansas Street
San Francisco, CA 94107
(415) 282-7600
e-mail: lhuang@actcm.edu
Web site: http://www.actcm.org
Accredited: 11/91

China International Medical University
Master of Science in Traditional Chinese Medicine
822 South Robertson Boulevard, Suite 300
Los Angeles, CA 90035
(310) 289-8394
e-mail: cimu@worldnet.att.net
Web site: http://www.home.att.net/~cimu

Dongguk Royal University
Master of Science in Oriental Medicine
440 South Shatto Place
Los Angeles, CA 90020
(213) 487-0110
e-mail: dru@pdc.net
Web site: http://www.dru.edu
Accredited: 5/94

Emperor's College of Traditional Oriental Medicine
Master of Traditional Oriental Medicine
1807-B Wilshire Boulevard
Santa Monica, CA 90403
(310) 453-8300
e-mail: dsl@emperors.edu
Web site: http://www.emperors.edu

Five Branches Institute: College of Traditional Chinese Medicine
Master of Traditional Chinese Medicine
200 7th Avenue
Santa Cruz, CA 95062
(831) 476-9424
e-mail: tcm@fivebranches.edu
Web site: http://www.fivebranches.edu
Accredited: 5/96

Kyung San University
Master of Science in Oriental Medicine
8322 Garden Grove Boulevard
Garden Grove, CA 92844
(714) 636-0337
e-mail: ohmsclinic@earthlink.net

Meiji College of Oriental Medicine
Master of Science in Oriental Medicine
2550 Shattuck Avenue
Berkeley, CA 94704
(510) 666-8248
e-mail: meiji@pacbell.net
Web site: http://www.meijicollege.org
Accredited: 5/98

Pacific College of Oriental Medicine at San Diego
Master of Science in Traditional Oriental Medicine
7445 Mission Valley Road, Suites 103–106
San Diego, CA 92108
(619) 574-6909
e-mail: jmiller@ormed.edu
Web site: http://www.ormed.edu

Samra University of Oriental Medicine
Master of Sciences in Oriental Medicine
3000 South Robertson Boulevard, 4th floor
Los Angeles, CA 90034
(310) 202-6444
e-mail: admissions@samra.edu
Web site: http://www.samra.edu

Santa Barbara College of Oriental Medicine
Master of Acupuncture and Oriental Medicine
1919 State Street, Suite 204
Santa Barbara, CA 93101
(805) 898-1180
e-mail: admissions@sbcom.edu
Web site: http://www.sbcom.edu

South Baylo University
Master of Science in Acupuncture and Oriental Medicine
1126 North Brookhurst Street
Anaheim, CA 92801
(714) 533-1495
e-mail: ron@southbaylo.edu
Web site: http://www.southbaylo.edu

South Baylo University, Los Angeles Branch
2727 West 6th Street
Los Angeles, CA 90015
(213) 738-0712

Yo San University of Traditional Chinese Medicine
Master of Acupuncture and Traditional Chinese Medicine
13315 W. Washington Boulevard
Los Angeles, CA 90066

(310) 577-3000
e-mail: info@yosan.edu
Web site: http://www.yosan.edu

COLORADO

Colorado School of Traditional Chinese Medicine
Master of Science in Oriental Medicine
1441 York Street, Suite 202
Denver, CO 80206-2127
(303) 329-6355
Web site: http://www.traditionalhealing.net

Southwest Acupuncture College
Master of Science in Oriental Medicine
6658 Gunpark Drive
Boulder, CO 80301
(303) 581-9955
e-mail: swacs@compuserve.com
Web site: http://www.swacupuncture.com

CONNECTICUT

College of Naturopathic Medicine
Master of Science in Acupuncture
Master of Acupuncture
University of Bridgeport
Health Sciences Center
60 Lafayette Avenue
Bridgeport, CT 06604
(800) 392-3582 ext. 4108
e-mail: admit@ubcom.bridgeport.edu
Web site: http://www.bridgeport.edu/acupunct

Connecticut Institute of Herbal Studies
Certificate of Completion of Chinese Herbology
Certificate of Completion of Traditional Chinese Theory
87 Market Square
Newington, CT 06111
(860) 666-5064
e-mail: laurachina@aol.com
Web site: http://www.ctherbschool.com

FLORIDA

Academy for Five Element Acupuncture
Master of Acupuncture
1170-A East Hallandale Beach Boulevard
Hallandale, FL 33009
(954) 456-6336
e-mail: AFEA@compuserve.com
Web site: http://www.acupuncturist.com

Academy of Chinese Healing Arts
Diploma in Oriental Medicine
513 South Orange Avenue
Sarasota, FL 34236
(941) 955-4456
e-mail: info@acha.net
Web site: http://www.acha.net
Accredited: 11/99; Next Review: Fall/03

Academy of Integrated Medicine
Tao Medical Institute
3380 Tamiami Trail, Suite B-1
Port Charlotte, FL 33952
(941) 764-7500

Acupuncture and Massage Institute of Florida
1425 NW 6th Street
Gainesville, FL 32601
(352) 373-4800

Atlantic Institute of Oriental Medicine
Master of Science in Oriental Medicine
1057 SE 17th Street
Fort Lauderdale, FL 33316-2116
(954) 463-3888
e-mail: atom@atom.edu
Web site: http://www.atom.edu
Accredited: 5/99; Next Review: Spring/02

Chinese Medicine Institute
8386-88 SW 40th Street
Miami, FL 33155
(305) 228-0380

Dragon Rises School of Oriental Medicine
502 NW 16th Avenue, Suite 2
Gainesville, FL 32601
(352) 371-2833
Web site: http://www.dragonrises.net

Florida Institute of Traditional Chinese Medicine
Diploma in Traditional Chinese Medicine
5335 66th Street North
St. Petersburg, FL 33709
(727) 546-6565
e-mail: fitcm@gte.net
Web site: http://www.fitcm.com

Florida College of Natural Health
Branch 1: 7925 NW 12th Street, Suite 201
Miami, FL 33126
(305) 597-9599
(800) 599-9599
e-mail: miami@fcnh.com

Branch 2: 1751 Mound Street, Suite G100
Sarasota, FL 34236
(941) 954-8999
(800) 966-7117
e-mail: sarasota@fcnh.com

Branch 3: 887 East Altamonte Drive
Altamonte Springs, FL 32701
(800) 393-7337
e-mail: orlando@fcnh.com

Branch 4: 2001 W. Sample Road, Suite 100
Pompano Beach, FL 33064
(954) 975-6400
(800) 541-9299

Han Tang School of Acupuncture and Oriental Medicine
3140 North Courtenay Parkway
Merritt Island, FL 32953
(321) 454-9259

Institute of Classical Acupuncture
107 SW 7th Street
Gainesville, FL 32601
(352) 378-5056

Mandarin School of Chinese Medicine
4237 Salisbury Road
Jacksonville, FL 32216
(904) 296-0906

National College of Oriental Medicine
Master in Oriental Medicine
7100 Lake Ellenor Drive
Orlando, FL 32809-5721
(407) 888-8689
e-mail: info@acupunctureschool.com
Web site: http://www.acupunctureschool.com
Reaccredited: 11/00; Next Review: Fall/03

Southeast Institute of Oriental Medicine
Diploma in Oriental Medicine
10506 North Kendall Drive
Miami, FL 33176
(305) 595-9500
e-mail: aai@acupuncture.pair.com
Web site: http://www.acupuncture.pair.com
Accredited: 11/00; Next Review: Fall/03

HAWAII

Institute of Clinical Acupuncture and Oriental Medicine
Master of Science in Oriental Medicine
1270 Queen Emma Street, Suite 107
Honolulu, HI 96813
(808) 521-2288
e-mail: info@orientalmedschool.com
Web site: http://www.orientalmedschool.com

Tai Hsuan Foundation College of Acupuncture and Herbal Medicine
Master of Acupuncture and Oriental Medicine
1110 University Avenue, Suite 309
Honolulu, HI 96826
(808) 949-1050
e-mail: taihsuancollege@cs.com
Accredited: 4/91

Traditional Chinese Medical College of Hawaii
Diploma in Oriental Medicine
65-1206 Mamalohoa Highway, Building 3, Suite 9
Kamuela, HI 96743
(808) 885-9226
e-mail: tcmch1@kona.net
Web site: http://www.kona.net/~chinese

ILLINOIS

Midwest College for Oriental Medicine
Certificate of Completion in Acupuncture
Master of Science in Oriental Medicine
4334 North Hazel, Suite 206
Chicago, IL 60613
(773) 975-1295
e-mail: info@acupuncture.edu
Web site: http://www.acupuncture.edu
Accredited: 11/93

Pacific College of Oriental Medicine
Master of Sciences in Traditional Oriental Medicine
3646 North Broadway, 2nd Floor
Chicago, IL 60613

(773) 477-4822
e-mail: jmiller@ormed.edu
Web site: http://www.ormed.edu
Accredited: 5/01

MARYLAND

Maryland Institute of Traditional Chinese Medicine
Diploma in Acupuncture
4641 Montgomery Avenue, Suite 415
Bethesda, MD 20814
(301) 718-7373
e-mail: admissions@mitcm.org
Web site: http://www.mitcm.org
Accredited: 5/98

Tai Sophia Institute
Master of Acupuncture
10227 Wincopin Circle, Suite 100
Columbia, MD 21044-3422
(301) 596-6006
e-mail: admissions@tai.edu
Accredited: 5/85

MASSACHUSETTS

New England School of Acupuncture
Masters in Acupuncture
40 Belmont Street
Watertown, MA 02472
(617) 926-1788
Web site: http://www.nesa.edu
Accredited: 2/88

MINNESOTA

Minnesota College of Acupuncture and Oriental Medicine
Master of Acupuncture
Master of Oriental Medicine
Northwestern Health Sciences University
2501 West 84th Street
Bloomington, MN 55431
(952) 888-4777
e-mail: miahs@nwhealth.edu
Web site: http://www.nwhealth.edu
Accredited: 5/99

NEW JERSEY

Eastern School of Acupuncture and Traditional Medicine
Diploma in Acupuncture
215 Glenridge Avenue
Montclair, NJ 07042
(973) 746-8717
e-mail: easternschoolacup@earthlink.net
Web site: http://www.easternschool.com

NEW MEXICO

International Institute of Chinese Medicine
Master of Oriental Medicine
Branch 1: P.O. Box 29988
Santa Fe, NM 87592-9988
(505) 473-5233
(800) 377-4561
e-mail: 102152.3463@compuserve.com
Web site: http://www.thuntek.net/iicm

Branch 2: 4600 Montgomery NE, Building 1, Suite 1
Albuquerque, NM 87109
(505) 883-5569
e-mail: panda@thuntek.net
Accredited: 11/90

Southwest Acupuncture College
Master of Science in Oriental Medicine
Branch 1: 2960 Rodeo Park Drive West
Santa Fe, NM 87505
(505) 438-8884
e-mail: swacs@compuserve.com
Web site: http://www.swacupuncture.com
Branch 2: 4308 Carlisle NE, Suite 205
Albuquerque, NM 87107
(505) 888-8898

NEW YORK

Mercy College Program in Acupuncture and Oriental Medicine
Master of Professional Studies in Acupuncture and
    Oriental Medicine
555 Broadway
Dobbs Ferry, NY 10522
(914) 674-7401
e-mail: acu@mercynet.edu
Web site: http://www.mercynet.edu/degreeprgms/
    gradprograms/acupuncture.cfm
Accredited: 11/00

New York College of Health Professions
Master of Science in Acupuncture and Oriental Medicine
Master of Science in Oriental Medicine
6801 Jericho Turnpike
Syosset, NY 11791-4465
(516) 364-0808
e-mail: nycinfo@nycollege.edu
Web site: http://www.nycollege.edu

New York Institute of Chinese Medicine
Diploma in Acupuncture
Diploma in Oriental Medicine
155 First Street
Mineola, NY 11501
(516) 739-1545

Pacific College of Oriental Medicine–New York
Master of Science of Acupuncture
Master of Science in Oriental Medicine
915 Broadway, 3rd Floor
New York, NY 10010
(212) 982-3456
e-mail: jmiller@ormed.edu
Web site: http://www.ormed.edu

Swedish Institute: School of Acupuncture and Oriental Studies
Diploma in Acupuncture
226 West 26th Street
P.O. Box 11130
New York, NY 10001
(212) 924-5900
e-mail: acupuncture@swedishinstitute.com
Web site: http://www.swedish-institute.com

Touro Of Acupuncture, Manhattan Campus
27-23 West 23rd Street
New York, NY 10010
(212) 463-0400, ext. 553
e-mail: om@touro.edu
Web site: http://www.touro.edu/orientalmedicine

Tri-State College of Acupuncture
Master of Science in Acupuncture
80 8th Avenue, 4th Floor
New York, NY 10011
(212) 242-2255
e-mail: tsitca@aol.com
Accredited: 11/93

NORTH CAROLINA
Atlantic University of Chinese Medicine
P.O. Box 790
Mars Hill, NC 28754
(877) 523-2826
(828) 689-1669
e-mail: information@aucm.com
Web site: http://www.aucm.com

Jung Tao School of Classical Chinese Medicine
207 Dale Adams Road
Sugar Grove, NC 28679
(828) 297-4181
e-mail: admissions@jungtao.edu
Web site: http://www.jungtao.edu

OREGON

National College of Naturopathic Medicine
Master of Science in Oriental Medicine
049 SW Porter
Portland, OR 97201
(503) 499-4343
e-mail: admissions@ncnm.edu
Web site: http://www.ncnm.edu

Oregon College of Oriental Medicine
Master of Acupuncture and Oriental Medicine
10525 SE Cherry Blossom Drive
Portland, OR 97216
(503) 253-3443
e-mail: 103226.164@compuserve.com
Web site: http://www.infinite.org/oregon.acupuncture

TEXAS

Academy of Oriental Medicine at Austin
Master of Science in Oriental Medicine
2700 West Anderson Lane, Suite 204
Austin, TX 78757
(512) 454-1188
e-mail: acuaoma@aol.com
Web site: http://www.aoma.edu

American College of Acupuncture and Oriental Medicine
Master of Science in Oriental Medicine
9100 Park West Drive
Houston, TX 77063
(713) 780-9777
e-mail: 102657.1730@compuserve.com
Web site: http://www.acaom.edu

Dallas Institute of Acupuncture and Oriental Medicine
Master of Science Degree in Oriental Medicine
2947 Walnut Hill Lane, Suite 101
Dallas, TX 75229
(214) 350-4282
e-mail: diaom@flash.net
Web site: http://www.diaom.com
Accredited: 5/01

Texas College of Traditional Chinese Medicine
Masters of Science in Oriental Medicine
4005 Manchaca Road, Suite 200
Austin, TX 78704
(512) 444-8082
e-mail: texastcm@texastcm.edu
Web site: http://www.texastcm.edu
Accredited: 11/96

WASHINGTON

Bastyr University
Master of Science in Acupuncture
Master of Science in Acupuncture and Oriental Medicine
14500 Juanita Drive NE
Kenmore, WA 98028
(425) 823-1300
e-mail: admiss@bastyr.edu
Web site: http://www.bastyr.edu
Accredited: 11/94

Northwest Institute of Acupuncture and Oriental Medicine
Master of Acupuncture
Master of Traditional Chinese Medicine
701 North 34th Street, Suite 300
Seattle, WA 98103
(206) 633-2419
e-mail: folks@niaom.edu
Web site: http://www.niaom.edu
Accredited: 4/90

Seattle Institute of Oriental Medicine
Master of Acupuncture and Oriental Medicine
916 NE 65th Street, Suite B
Seattle, WA 98115
(206) 517-4541
e-mail: info@siom.com
Web site: http://www.siom.com
Accredited: 5/98

WISCONSIN

Midwest College for Oriental Medicine
Certificate of Completion in Acupuncture
Master of Science in Oriental Medicine
6226 Bankers Road, Suites 5 and 6
Racine, WI 53403
(262) 554-2010
e-mail: info@acupuncture.edu
Web site: http://www.acupuncture.edu
Accredited: 11/93

Wisconsin Institute of Chinese Herbology
Certificate in Chinese Herbology
Diploma in Massage (entitles graduate to state licensure as a massage therapist in Wisconsin; incorporates Western and Oriental bodywork therapy techniques)
5200 Washington Avenue, Suite 220
Racine, WI 53405
(262) 619-1590
e-mail: herbstudys@aol.com

CANADA

Academy of Classical Oriental Sciences
303 Vernon Street
Nelson, BC V1L 4E3
(250) 352-5887
(888) 333-8868
e-mail: acos@acos.org
Web site: http://www.acos.org

Canadian College of Acupuncture and Oriental Medicine
855 Cormorant Street
Victoria, BC V8W 1R2
(250) 384-2942
e-mail: ccaom@islandnet.com
Web site: http://www.ccaom.com/index.html

Grant MacEwan College
Health and Community Studies Division, Acupuncture
City Centre Campus
Room 7-367, 10700 - 104 Avenue
Edmonton, AB T5J 4S2
(780) 497-4736
Web site: http://www.gmcc.ab.ca/

**International College of Traditional Chinese Medicine
of Vancouver**
1508 W. Broadway, Suite 201
Vancouver, BC V6J 1W8
(604) 731-2926
e-mail: info@tcmcollege.com
Web site: http://tcmcollege.com

Michener Institute of Applied Health Sciences
Diploma in Acupuncture program
222 St. Patrick Street
Toronto, ON M5T 1V4
(416) 596-3101
Web site: http://www.michener.on.ca
Candidacy granted: 5/00

Tzu Chi Institute for Complementary and Alternative Medicine
715 West 12th Avenue
Health Centre, 4th Floor West
Vancouver, BC V5Z 1M9
(604) 875-4769

National Organizations

**American Association of Acupuncture and Oriental
Medicine (AAAOM)**
4101 Lake Boone Trail, Suite 201
Raleigh, NC 27607
(919) 787-5181
Professional national organization which provides a list
of local members.

National Certification Commission for Acupuncture and Oriental Medicine
11 Canal Center Plaza, Suite 300
Alexandria, VA 22314
(703) 548-9004
Web site: http://www.nccaom.org
The main organization that is connected to most state licensing institutions. The NCCAOM offers a test that most states use to verify basic competency in acupuncture.

Alexander Technique Organizations

Alexander Technique International (ATI)
Web site: http://www.ati-net.com/
The ATI is a worldwide professional organization for the Alexander Technique. Its Web site offers general information on the Alexander Technique, an up-to-date international listing of ATI teachers, training, and upcoming Alexander Technique workshops and events, articles on learning and teaching the technique, a resource section covering books, journals, audio tapes, videotapes, articles, and related links.

Urbana-Champaign Teachers of the Alexander Technique
Web site: http://www.prairienet.org/alexandertech
The Urbana-Champaign Teachers of the Alexander Technique is an informal affiliation of certified teachers. Its Web site provides information on the Alexander Technique.

For Further Reading

Becker, Robert O. *Cross Currents: The Promise of Electromedicine, the Perils of Electropollution.* New York: Putnam, 1991.

Beinfield, Harriet, and Efrem Korngold. *Between Heaven and Earth: A Guide to Chinese Medicine.* New York: Random House, 1992.

Brennan, Barbara Ann. *Hands of Light: A Guide to Healing through the Human Energy Field.* New York: Bantam Doubleday Dell, 1988.

Chopra, Deepak. *Quantum Healing: Exploring the Frontiers of Mind/Body Medicine.* New York: Bantam Doubleday Dell, 1990.

Ferguson, Marilyn. *The Aquarian Conspiracy: Personal and Social Transformation In Our Time,* Vol. 1. New York: Putnam, 1981.

Frawley, David. *Ayurvedic Healing: A Comprehensive Guide.* Twin Lakes, WI: Lotus Press, 2000.

Gaynor, Mitchell L. *The Sounds of Healing: A Physician Reveals the Therapeutic Power of Sound, Voice, and Music.* New York: Broadway Books, 1999.

Gerber, Richard. *Vibrational Medicine: The #1 Handbook for Subtle-Energy Therapies.* Rochester, NY: Inner Traditions International, 2001.

Hay, Louise. *You Can Heal Your Life.* Carlsbad, CA: Hay House, 1999.

Murphy, Michael. *Future of the Body: Explorations into the Further Evolution of Human Nature.* New York: Putnam, 1993.

Myss, Caroline. *Why People Don't Heal and How They Can.* New York: Crown Publishing Group, 1998.

Santopietro, Nancy. *Feng Shui: Harmony by Design.* New York: Berkley Publishing, 1996.

Index

A

About Massage (Web site), 123-124

Academy of Natural Healing, 76

Accreditation Commission for Acupuncture and Oriental Medicine, 46

acupuncture/ acupuncturists, 5, 6, 7, 9, 16, 25, 34, 70, 72, 73, 78, 83, 96, 103, 107, 122, 137, 154
explanation of, 42
growth of, 46
how it works, 43-46
schools for, 5, 8, 46-47, 118

Alexander, Frederick Matthias, 61

Alexander Technique, 61-63, 65

alternative medicine, definition of, 6

Alternative Medicine Network, 131-132

Alternative Medicine University (Web site), 124

American Osteopathic Association, 60

American Polarity Therapy Association, 103-104

Andrews, Lynn, 106

antibiotics, overuse of, 14-15

Aquarian Conspiracy, The, 126-127

aromatherapy, 5, 53, 83, 84-85, 122, 124

About the Author

Alan Steinfeld is a nationally certified acupuncturist with a master's degree in Oriental medicine. His approach to healing combines acupuncture with bodywork, emotional release, dietary counseling, herbology, and shamanic practices from many different traditions around the world.

Along with a private practice, Steinfeld also hosts and produces the New York area (Channel 57) cable television program *New Realities TV*. Each week the show investigates the principles of body, mind, and spirit integration. Currently, there are over 300 guests in the program's catalogue. Please check the *New Realities* Web site, http://www.newrealitiestv.com, for a complete catalogue of topics and guests.

Steinfeld also has published a series of articles on meta-biology and evolution for *The Golden Thread* magazine in Washington State. He is the co-author of the theatrical piece "Quintessence," based on many of the holistic and alchemical principles found in this book.

The author lives and works in New York City, but often travels to other parts of the world to increase his knowledge of the human experience. He believes the future of the planet depends upon the acceptance of new realities that prove we are part of a greater consciousness. To contact the author, e-mail him at alan@newrealitiestv.com.